TAXATION:
THE PEOPLE'S BUSINESS

THE MACMILLAN COMPANY
NEW YORK · BOSTON · CHICAGO · DALLAS
ATLANTA · SAN FRANCISCO

MACMILLAN & CO., Limited
LONDON · BOMBAY · CALCUTTA
MELBOURNE

THE MACMILLAN CO. OF CANADA, Ltd.
TORONTO

TAXATION:
THE PEOPLE'S BUSINESS

BY
ANDREW W. MELLON

New York
THE MACMILLAN COMPANY
1924

PREFACE

Many of the views on taxation herein expressed have appeared from time to time in letters to Committees of Congress and to various organizations and individuals. It has seemed worth while to collect these views and publish them in a compact form, to which are appended also various tables and documents of possible interest to students of taxation. I am indebted to *The Forum* magazine, *The Independent,* and others for permission to publish excerpts from articles. I also wish to express my indebtedness to Mr. S. Parker Gilbert, former Under Secretary of the Treasury, and to the Under Secretary of the Treasury, Mr. Garrard B. Winston, for the invaluable assistance which he has rendered not only in the preparation of this book but in the conduct of the public business of the Treasury.

A. W. MELLON.

Washington,
April, 1924.

CONTENTS

CHAPTER		PAGE
I	Fundamental Principles	9
II	Treasury Policies	25
III	Revising the Taxes	51
IV	Surtaxes	69
V	Taxing Energy and Initiative . .	93
VI	Estate Taxes	111
VII	Benefits of Tax Reduction . . .	127
VIII	Tax-Exempt Securities	141
	Appendix	175

CHAPTER I

FUNDAMENTAL PRINCIPLES

TAXATION: THE PEOPLE'S BUSINESS

CHAPTER I

FUNDAMENTAL PRINCIPLES

THE problem of the Government is to fix rates which will bring in a maximum amount of revenue to the Treasury and at the same time bear not too heavily on the taxpayer or on business enterprises. A sound tax policy must take into consideration three factors. It must produce sufficient revenue for the Government; it must lessen, so far as possible, the burden of taxation on those least able to bear it; and it must also remove those influences which might retard the continued steady development of business and industry on which, in the last analysis, so much of our prosperity depends. Furthermore, a perma-

9

nent tax system should be designed not merely for one or two years nor for the effect it may have on any given class of taxpayers, but should be worked out with regard to conditions over a long period and with a view to its ultimate effect on the prosperity of the country as a whole.

These are the principles on which the Treasury's tax policy is based, and any revision of taxes which ignores these fundamental principles will prove merely a makeshift and must eventually be replaced by a system based on economic, rather than political, considerations.

There is no reason why the question of taxation should not be approached from a non-partisan and business viewpoint. In recent years, in any discussion of tax revision, the question which has caused most controversy is the proposed reduction of the surtaxes. Yet recommendations for such reductions have not been confined to either Republican or Democratic administrations. My own recommendations on this subject were in line with similar ones made by Secretaries Houston and Glass, both of whom served under a Democratic President. Tax revision should never be made the football either of partisan or class politics but should be worked out by those who have made a careful study of the subject in its larger aspects and are prepared to recommend the course which, in the end, will prove for the country's best interest.

I have never viewed taxation as a means of rewarding one class of taxpayers or punishing another. If such a point of view ever controls our public policy, the traditions of freedom, justice and equality of opportunity, which are the distinguishing characteristics of our American civilization, will have disappeared and in their place we shall have class legislation with all its attendant evils. The man who seeks to perpetuate prejudice and class hatred is doing America an ill service. In attempting to promote or to defeat legislation by arraying one class of taxpayers against another, he shows a complete misconception of those principles of equality on which the country was founded. Any man of energy and initiative in this country can get what he wants out of life. But when that initiative is crippled by legislation or by a tax system which denies him the right to receive a reasonable share of his earnings, then he will no longer exert himself and the country will be deprived of the energy on which its continued greatness depends.

This condition has already begun to make itself felt as a result of the present unsound basis of taxation. The existing tax system is an inheritance from the war. During that time the highest taxes ever levied by any country were borne uncomplainingly by the American people for the purpose of defraying the unusual and ever-increasing expenses incident to the successful conduct of a great war. Normal tax rates were increased, and a system of surtaxes was evolved in order to make the man of large income pay more proportionately than the smaller taxpayer. If he had twice as much income, he paid not twice, but three or four times as much tax. For a short time the surtaxes yielded a large revenue. But since the close of the war people have come to look upon them as a business expense and have treated them accordingly by avoiding payment as much as possible. The history of taxation shows that taxes which are inherently excessive are not paid. The high rates inevitably put pressure upon the taxpayer to withdraw his capital from productive business and invest it in tax-exempt securities or to find other lawful methods of avoiding the realization of taxable income. The result is that the sources of taxation are drying up; wealth is failing to carry its share of the tax burden; and capital is being diverted into channels which yield neither revenue to the Government nor profit to the people.

Before the period of the war, taxes as high as those now in effect would have been thought fantastic and impossible of payment. As a result of the patriotic desire of the people to contribute to the limit to the successful prosecution of the war, high taxes were assessed and ungrudgingly paid. Upon the conclusion of peace and the gradual removal of war-time conditions of business, the opportunity is presented to Congress to make the tax structure of the United States conform more closely to normal conditions and to remove the inequalities in that structure which directly injure our prosperity and cause strains upon our economic fabric. There is no question of the fact that if the country is to go forward in the future as it has in the past, we must make sure that all retarding influences are removed.

Adam Smith, in his great work, "Wealth of Nations," laid down as the first maxim of taxation that "The subjects of every state ought to contribute toward the support of the Government, as nearly as possible, in proportion to their respective abilities," and in his fourth and last maxim, that "Every tax ought to be so contrived as both to take out and to keep out of the pockets of the people as little as possible over and above what it brings into the public treasury of the state,'' citing as one of the ways by which this last maxim is violated a tax which ''may obstruct the industry of the people, and discourage them from applying to certain branches of business which might give maintenance and employment to great multitudes. . . . While it obliges the people to pay, it may thus diminish, or perhaps destroy, some of the funds, which might enable them more easily to do so.''

The further experience of one hundred and fifty years since this was written has emphasized the truth of these maxims, but those who argue against a reduction of surtaxes to more nearly peace-time figures cite only the first maxim, and ignore the fourth. The principle that a man should pay taxes in accordance with his ''ability to pay'' is sound but, like all other general statements, has its practical limitations and qualifications, and when, as a result of an excessive or unsound basis of taxation, it becomes evident that the source of taxation is drying

up and wealth is being diverted into unproductive channels, yielding neither revenue
to the Government nor profit to the people,
then it is time to readjust our basis of taxation upon sound principles.

It seems difficult for some to understand
that high rates of taxation do not necessarily
mean large revenue to the Government, and
that more revenue may often be obtained by
lower rates. There was an old saying that
a railroad freight rate should be "what the
traffic will bear"; that is, the highest rate at
which the largest quantity of freight would
move. The same rule applies to all private
businesses. If a price is fixed too high, sales
drop off and with them profits; if a price is
fixed too low, sales may increase, but again
profits decline. The most outstanding recent
example of this principle is the sales policy
of the Ford Motor Car Company. Does any
one question that Mr. Ford has made more
money by reducing the price of his car and
increasing his sales than he would have
made by maintaining a high price and a

greater profit per car, but selling less cars? The Government is just a business, and can and should be run on business principles.

Experience has shown that the present high rates of surtax are bringing in each year progressively less revenue to the Government. This means that the price is too high to the large taxpayer and he is avoiding a taxable income by the many ways which are available to him. What rates will bring in the largest revenue to the Government experience has not yet developed, but it is estimated that by cutting the surtaxes in half, the Government, when the full effect of the reduction is felt, will receive more revenue from the owners of large incomes at the lower rates of tax than it would have received at the higher rates. This is simply an application of the same business principle referred to above, just as Mr. Ford makes more money out of pricing his cars at $380 than at $3,000.

Looking at the subject, therefore, solely

from the standpoint of Government revenues, lower surtax rates are essential. If we consider, however, the far more important subject of the effect of the present high surtax rates on the development and prosperity of our country, then the necessity for a change is more apparent. The most noteworthy characteristic of the American people is their initiative. It is this spirit which has developed America, and it was the same spirit in our soldiers which made our armies successful abroad. If the spirit of business adventure is killed, this country will cease to hold the foremost position in the world. And yet it is this very spirit which excessive surtaxes are now destroying. Any one at all in touch with affairs knows of his own knowledge of buildings which have not been built, of businesses which have not been started, and of new projects which have been abandoned, all for the one reason—high surtaxes. If failure attends, the loss is borne exclusively by the adventurer, but if success ensues, the Government takes more than half of the profits. People argue the risk is not worth the return.

With the open invitation to all men who have wealth to be relieved from taxation by the simple expedient of investing in the more than $12,000,000,000 of tax-exempt securities now available, and which would be unaffected by any Constitutional amendment, the rich need not pay taxes. We violate Adam Smith's first maxim. Where these high surtaxes do bear, is not on the man who has acquired and holds available wealth, but on the man who, through his own initiative, is making wealth. The idle man is relieved; the producer is penalized. We violate the fourth maxim. We do not reach the people in proportion to their ability to pay and we destroy the initiative which produces the wealth in which the whole country should share, and which is the source of revenue to the Government.

In considering any reduction the Government must always be assured that taxes will not be so far reduced as to deprive the Treasury of sufficient revenue with which properly to run its business with the manifold activities now a part of the Federal Government and to take care of the public debt. Tax reduction must come out of surplus revenue. In determining the amount of surplus available these factors control: the revenue remaining the same, an increase in expenditures reduces the surplus, and expenditures remaining the same, anything which reduces the revenue reduces the surplus. The reaction, therefore, of the authorization of extraordinary or unsound expenditures is twofold—it serves, first, to raise the expenditures and so narrow the margin of available surplus; and, second, to decrease further or obliterate entirely this margin by a reduction of the Treasury's revenues through the disturbance of general business, which is promptly reflected in the country's income. On the other hand, a decrease of taxes causes an inspiration to trade and commerce which increases the prosperity of the country so that the revenues of the Government, even on a lower basis of tax, are increased. Taxation can be reduced to a point apparently in excess of the estimated surplus, because by the cumulative effect of such reduction, expenses remaining the same, a greater revenue is obtained.

High taxation, even if levied upon an economic basis, affects the prosperity of the country, because in its ultimate analysis the burden of all taxes rests only in part upon the individual or property taxed. It is largely borne by the ultimate consumer. High taxation means a high price level and high cost of living. A reduction in taxes, therefore, results not only in an immediate saving to the individual or property directly affected, but an ultimate saving to all people in the country. It can safely be said, that a reduction in the income tax reduces expenses not only of the income taxpayers but of the entire 110,000,000 people in the United States. It is for this basic reason that the present question of tax reform is not how much each individual taxpayer reduces his direct contribution, although this, of course, is a powerful influence upon the individual affected; the real problem to determine is what plan results in the least burden to the people and the most revenue to the Government.

CHAPTER II

TREASURY POLICIES

CHAPTER II

SINCE the war two guiding principles have dominated the financial policy of the Government. One is the balancing of the budget, and the other is the payment of the public debt. Both are in line with the fundamental policy of the Government since its beginning.

Alexander Hamilton, whose genius was responsible for the establishment of our financial system, early committed this Government to a policy of debt payment and keeping expenditures within income. "It will be the truest policy of the United States," he said, "to give all possible energy to public credit by a firm adherence to its strictest maxims; and yet, to avoid the ills of an excessive employment of it, by true economy and system in the public expenditure, by steadily cultivating peace, and by using sincere, efficient and persevering endeavors to diminish present debts, prevent the accumulation of new and secure the discharge, within a reasonable period, of such as it may be at any time a matter of necessity to contract.''

In accordance with this policy the nation from the very beginning began to pay its debts. Under Hamilton's leadership the debts incurred by the various States in the prosecution of the Revolutionary War were assumed by the new nation then struggling into existence, and immediate provisions were made for funding and gradually liquidating these obligations. Hamilton proposed a sinking fund, through whose operation, with later modifications, the debt was discharged within a reasonable number of years.

The policy thus inaugurated has been adhered to by succeeding administrations. Out of surplus revenues the public debt has been gradually paid off, so that at the time of our entrance into the World War, in April, 1917, the net public debt was slightly more than one billion dollars. The United States fol-

The cost of a great war, however, cannot be borne entirely by taxes. It must be financed in part by credit, which can be accomplished by long-time loans. In this way, the burden can be distributed over a term of years in such a way that too great payment does not fall on the taxpayers of any one year. Throughout its history the United States has followed the policy laid down by Hamilton of so funding the public debt that it can be liquidated without undue hardship. At the same time, the policy has been strictly adhered to that expenditures for the ordinary operations of the Government must be discharged out of current receipts raised from taxes. Part of the public debt must be paid each year out of current revenues, and such debt as is not paid off must be refunded and the whole eventually extinguished by paying from year to year the amounts accumulated in the sinking fund. The amount of the yearly payments must be determined by the taxes levied for the purpose, and the rate of taxation should at no time be so excessive as to discourage the hope of gain on the part of the individual taxpayer.

Many people cling to the old policy that debt retirement is bad for business, being the reverse of inflated conditions accompanying vast borrowings. They hold that new borrowings with reduced taxes are preferable to higher taxes with reduced debts. But a moment's reflection will convince any one that prosperity cannot come from continued plunging into debt. The present condition of Germany is the best proof of the danger of inflation and financial pyramiding. As a matter of fact, orderly debt retirement out of surplus revenues is better calculated to restore prosperity, for the debt is retired by taxes paid in for the purpose and the money retained for the payment of such taxes is saved from being dissipated in useless expenditure. The payment of debts is particularly desirable when the nation's obligations, as in the case of the United States, are owed to its own people. All payments of interest and principal are put back into circulation within the country. It may seem to be taking money out of one pocket in the form of taxes and putting it back in the other pocket in the guise of interest and part payment of the principal on bonds. But there are two distinctions to be noted: (1) not every taxpayer owns bonds, hence it is an advantage for the Government no longer to support the bondholders by the payment of interest collected as taxes from the nation at large; (2) the payments of principal on bonds are in sums that will find their way back into capital investments, whereas, if no payments are made and taxes remain uncollected, this amount will be dissipated as income in useless expenditures.

The United States has followed a sound policy in regard to payment of the war debt. It has appropriated annually a sum in excess of interest charges, the surplus being devoted to the reduction of the principal of the debt. The keynote of its policy in this regard, as the late President Harding stated in his first address to Congress, has been "or-

derly funding and gradual liquidation.'' In
the five full fiscal years since the end of hos-
tilities in the World War, the Government
has been able to balance its budget and the
Treasury has therefore been in the position
to make important progress within the same
period in the handling of the war debt. On
April 30, 1921, when the Treasury announced
its refunding program, the gross public debt
amounted to about 24 billion dollars, of which
over 7½ billion dollars was short-dated debt
maturing within about two years. The Treasury was faced with the necessity not only of
relieving business of the heavy tax burden
imposed during the war but also of retiring
or refunding the early maturing debt without disturbance to business and industry.

The Treasury completed during the fiscal
year ending June 30, 1923, the first phase of
its refunding program, and by the end of the
year all of the $7,500,000,000 of short-dated
debt maturing during the previous two and
one-half years had been either retired or refunded into more manageable maturities.

Except for the issue of about $750,000,000 of 25-30 year Treasury bonds in the fall of 1922, the refunding has all been on a short-term basis, and it has been arranged with a view to distributing the early maturities of debt at convenient intervals over the period before the maturity of the third Liberty Loan in 1928 in such manner that surplus revenues may be applied most effectively to the gradual reduction of the debt. With this object in view all of the short-term notes issued in the course of the refunding have been given maturities on quarterly tax-payment dates, and all outstanding issues of Treasury certificates have likewise been reduced to tax maturities.

The following table shows in summary form the distribution of the interest-bearing debt by maturities at various dates since August 31, 1919, when the gross debt reached the peak. From this table it will be seen that on March 31, 1924, the public debt had been reduced nearly five billion dollars from its highest point in 1919. In place of the old

INTEREST-BEARING DEBT, DISTRIBUTED BY MATURITIES, AND TOTAL GROSS DEBT AUGUST 31, 1919, TO MARCH 31, 1924

(*Millions of dollars*)

DATE	MATURING WITHIN FIVE YEARS				MATURING AFTER FIVE YEARS	TOTAL INTEREST-BEARING DEBT	TOTAL GROSS DEBT
	Within one year	One year to two years	Two years to five years	Total within five years [1]			
Aug. 31, 1919 . . .	4,201	. . . .	5,045	9,246	17,103	26,349	26,594
Apr. 30, 1921 . . .	2,820	572	4,209	7,602	16,158	23,760	23,994
June 30, 1921 . . .	2,699	4,494	425	7,618	16,119	23,737	23,976
June 30, 1922 . . .	4,336	366	2,044	6,746	15,965	22,711	22,964
June 30, 1923 . . .	1,393	1,432	2,647	5,473	16,535	22,008	22,350
Mar. 31, 1924 . . .	2,056	1,334	4,937	8,327	13,029	21,356	21,624

[1] Exclusive of interest-bearing obligations redeemable at the pleasure of the Government but not maturing within the period covered.

short-dated debt, there has been substituted
a new class of short-dated debt, aggregating
on March 31, 1924, about $8,327,000,000, ma-
turing within five years from that date.

This Government has followed the sound
policy of balancing its budget from year to
year, ordinary receipts against ordinary expenditures, and including as ordinary expenditures for budget purposes the sinking fund
and other debt retirements properly chargeable against ordinary receipts. This means
that provision must be made for expenditures
on account of interest and retirement of the
war debt before the Budget can balance; and
a balanced budget each year indicates a reasonable amount of debt retirement out of current revenues. To do otherwise would, of
course, make a farce of the sinking fund, for
on any other basis purchases of obligations
for retirement on this account would accomplish no debt retirement whatever and would
mean simply a shifting of borrowing from
one form to another.

Under the Budget system it is now possible for the Treasury to know in advance approximately the aggregate of expenditures for which it must provide funds during the year. To become completely effective the Budget should embrace all Government expenditures, including those which, in the guise of revolving funds and indefinite appropriations, do not now appear in the Budget at all.

The Budget cannot reflect the true state of Government finances until Congress puts an end to the practice, initiated during the war, of authorizing expenditures by means of indefinite or revolving-fund appropriations. The Constitution expressly provides that "no money shall be drawn from the Treasury but in consequence of appropriations made by law; and a regular statement of the receipts and expenditures of all public money shall be published from time to time." This Constitutional requirement has been evaded by diverting Government funds before they are covered into the Treasury. At the same time the Treasury is rendered unable to perform its Constitutional function of publishing "a regular statement of the receipts and expenditures of all public money."

Such indefinite appropriations not only conceal how much money is being spent, but frequently conceal even the fact of an appropriation being made. By means of indirect and indefinite appropriations of this character, hundreds of millions are spent which, if a direct appropriation were necessary, could never be authorized. In fact the practice has reached such proportions as to be a matter of grave concern, and it was vigorously denounced by President Harding in one of his annual messages. It has become the first principle of strategy on the part of people interested in appropriations for various special purposes to frame the matter so as to authorize the use of the public funds indirectly, or in indefinite terms, or by authorizations for expenditure of unexpended balances, perhaps appropriated originally for other purposes, or by authorizations to divert Government receipts before they ever reach the

Treasury. In order to accomplish this end efforts are made to find general words which do not speak in terms of appropriations and cannot be readily calculated.

However necessary these practices may have been during the war in order to give greater freedom of administrative action in the use of public funds, they are utterly indefensible in time of peace. By diverting funds before they reach the Treasury, Congress is creating the dangerous precedent of allowing Government money to be expended without the direct control of Congress or the supervision of the Treasury. The disposition of vast funds is put into the hands of administrative officers of various departments or Government agencies, without limitations as to their use; and a situation is thus created which not only is contrary to the intent of the Constitution but is also unscientific and dangerous in the extreme.

Throughout the world, the process of deflation has been retarded by the system of subsidies prevalent in so many countries. The war left in its train many economic hardships. Many classes of producers suffered from lack of demand for their products, while the consuming classes were forced to pay extortionate prices for articles in which a scarcity existed, such as houses, bread and coal. Various measures have been taken to remedy these conditions. Subsidies have been granted to some industries to encourage production until the demand should become normal; and bonuses have been granted to relieve certain classes of consumers burdened by the high prices of necessaries. Such efforts to regulate the law of supply and demand have generally proved ineffective, and in many European countries have resulted in expenditures by the state for which no adequate income could be found.

A bonus or subsidy can be paid only by taking money out of the pockets of all the people in order that it shall find its way back into the pockets of some of the people. It accomplishes nothing less than a redistribution of the wealth of the country by governmental operation, and constitutes a bad precedent, which is likely to prove more and more expensive to the country with each surrender to organized pressure.

It is of the utmost importance that expenditures should be kept down to the minimum requirements of the Government and that the Budget should balance, for, in a world of disordered governmental finances, the United States owes it to itself to keep its house in order and balance its Budget as it has done in the last five years.

The aggregate of Government expenditures subject to modification by executive control is comparatively small in amount. Such items as payment of the public debt, trust fund investments, pensions, appropriations for Indians, Customs and Internal Revenue, and, for the most part, veterans' relief cannot be reduced by the executive departments. The attached table (Appendix F), shows the large amount of fixed charges which the Government must meet each year.

The diagrams on pages 42, 43 present in

graphic form the percentage distribution of receipts and expenditures for the fiscal year 1923 and may be taken as fairly typical of conditions which the Government is facing in the next few years.

The Government's expenditures may be divided into two classes, as follows:

Class 1.

War Department	10.62%
Navy Department	9.01%
Sinking Fund and other debt retirements	10.89%
Interest on the public debt	28.56%
Veterans' Bureau	12.49%
Pensions	7.19%
Total	78.76%

Class 2.

Trust fund investments	.95%
Indians	1.22%
Refunds	4.17%
Good roads	2.15%
Operations in special accounts	1.33%
All other expenditures	11.42%
Total	21.24%

From the above, it will be seen that wars, past and future, are responsible for the consumption of over three-fourths of the public revenue. It is time to face the facts and recognize that, in spite of the utmost economy that can be effected in administration, the

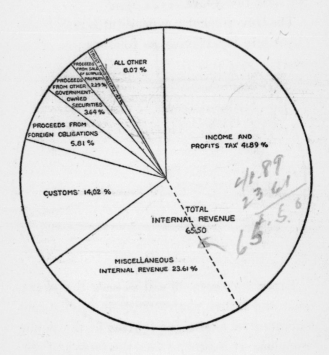

DIAGRAM I

ORDINARY RECEIPTS OF THE GOVERNMENT
FISCAL YEAR ENDED JUNE 30, 1923

TOTAL = $ 4,007,135,481.

ALL OTHER
8.07 %

PROCEEDS FROM SALE OF SURPLUS PROPERTY 1.87 %

PROCEEDS FROM OTHER GOVERNMENT OWNED SECURITIES 2.29 %
3.64 %

PROCEEDS FROM FOREIGN OBLIGATIONS
5.81 %

CUSTOMS 14.02 %

INCOME AND PROFITS TAX 41.89 %

TOTAL
INTERNAL REVENUE
65.50

MISCELLANEOUS
INTERNAL REVENUE 23.61 %

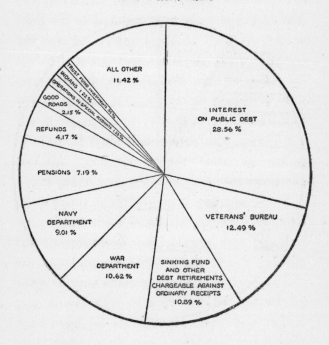

DIAGRAM 2

GOVERNMENT EXPENDITURES CHARGEABLE AGAINST
ORDINARY RECEIPTS
FISCAL YEAR ENDED JUNE 30, 1923

TOTAL = $ 3,697,478,020

ALL OTHER
11.42 %

TRUST FUND INVESTMENTS 3.27 %

INDIANS 1.22 %

OPERATIONS IN SPECIAL ACCOUNTS 1.33 %

GOOD
ROADS
2.15 %

REFUNDS
4.17 %

PENSIONS 7.19 %

NAVY
DEPARTMENT
9.01 %

WAR
DEPARTMENT
10.62 %

SINKING FUND
AND OTHER
DEBT RETIREMENTS
CHARGEABLE AGAINST
ORDINARY RECEIPTS
10.89 %

VETERANS' BUREAU
12.49 %

INTEREST
ON PUBLIC DEBT
28.56 %

cost of government cannot be greatly reduced so long as wars continue to recur with their aftermath of vastly increased expenditures.

Class 2 on page 41 shows where reductions in expenditures must be made. The Army and Navy have already been reduced to the limit consistent with national safety. From the comparatively small amount devoted to the operation of the Government departments, only a limited amount can be saved; and if any drastic reduction is to be made in expenditures, the public debt must be paid in order to stop the tremendous interest charges which are paid each year out of taxes.

There are two means of debt retirement; first, repayments on loans made to foreign nations, and second, the operation of the Sinking Fund. As regards foreign loans, the law authorizes that repayments may be made in United States Government bonds and notes; and such repayments as have been received to date from Great Britain have been almost entirely in Liberty Bonds, which are accepted at par and accrued interest in payment of an equal amount of foreign debt. The Liberty Bonds received in this way by the United States Government are immediately cancelled and a corresponding reduction made both in the foreign debt and in the public debt of the United States. The transaction is merely a paper one and brings no revenue into the Treasury.

It is absolutely necessary that a sound policy of debt retirement be followed and that repayments of the "foreign loans" be applied in reduction of the debt owed by the United States to the holders of Liberty Bonds. The Victory Liberty Loan Act provided for a "Sinking Fund" or annual appropriation which, added to repayments received from foreign governments, would retire the public debt within a reasonable period.

The money represented by these loans to foreign governments was borrowed in the first place by the United States from its own citizens, to whom Liberty Bonds and Victory Notes were given in exchange. The funds, as everyone knows, have already been spent by the foreign debtor nations in the successful prosecution of the war, and, when these funds are repaid to this Government, the latter must, in honesty to the holders of Liberty Bonds, buy up and cancel those bonds; or, if repayments are made by foreign governments in the form of Liberty Bonds, then these securities, which cannot be reissued, must be retired and the public debt reduced by a corresponding amount.

In view of the great carrying charge of the debt, it would seem imperative that the debt be reduced as rapidly as possible and that no further obligations be incurred in the form of unusual or extraordinary expenditures. In so far as this Government is concerned, its policy has been to keep its own house in order, to maintain the gold standard unimpaired, to balance its budget and to carry out a reasonable program for the orderly funding and gradual liquidation of the war debt. It is becoming more and more apparent that the gradual restoration of business and industry in Europe will come not only through the maintenance of sound financial conditions in this country but also in the gradual adoption of similar principles by the governments of Europe, many of which still persist in policies of budgetary deficits and currency inflation.

CHAPTER III

REVISING THE TAXES

CHAPTER III

REVISING THE TAXES

A COROLLARY of Hamilton's policy of keeping the Government's expenditures within its income is the further policy of keeping the revenues not too greatly in excess of expenditures. It was in accordance with this policy that the Treasury in the fall of 1923 recommended a reduction of the taxes.

Theories of taxation are more interesting and more intelligible when applied to actual conditions for, in the conduct of government, as every responsible official sooner or later finds out, one is more often confronted with a condition than with a theory. It will be worth while, therefore, to review the recommendations made by the Treasury in connection with conditions existing at the end of the fiscal year 1923.

The fiscal years 1922 and 1923 each closed

with a surplus of about three hundred and ten million dollars above all expenditures, chargeable against ordinary receipts, including the Sinking Fund and other similar retirements of the debt. This surplus, of course, was not, as many seemed to think, a deposit of cash in bank, available for immediate expenditure. The public debt at the close of the fiscal year 1923 was about twenty-two billion dollars, and of this amount one billion dollars was in short-time certificates, having a maturity of less than a year; and four billion dollars was in notes maturing within four years. On each of the four quarterly tax payment dates the Government issues its Treasury Certificates to keep stable the money market during tax payments and to give the Government sufficient funds with which to operate until the next payment. In other words, at least four times a year the Government borrows money and pays it back out of tax receipts. An excess, therefore, of receipts over expenditures for any three months' period simply results in smaller borrowing for the next period, and does not result in an accumulation of cash. It is an automatic reduction of the debt. The Government operates in the same manner as does a business man who is heavily in debt to the bank. The latter merely renews his paper for lesser amounts each ninety days as he accumulates funds with which to pay off his notes.

In the case of the Government, therefore, every new expenditure must be paid out of new borrowings. The Sinking Fund, which is part of the Budget of regular governmental expenditures, reduces the debt by about three hundred million dollars a year, and the British repayments and other less important items bring the amount of debt reduction annually to about half a billion dollars. These repayments will eliminate the debt within a reasonable period; and the Treasury felt that the desirability of further debt reduction out of surplus receipts was not so great as a lessening of the tax burden. Based upon these premises, what was known as the Mellon Plan of tax reduction was worked out.

In view not only of the surplus but of the heavy and unscientific tax rates in force at the close of the fiscal year 1923, the Treasury felt that the fortunate condition of the finances offered an opportunity not merely to reduce the taxes but to revise the system in accordance with sound principles of taxation. In a letter which I wrote on November 10, 1923, to Honorable William R. Green, Acting Chairman of the Committee on Ways and Means of the House of Representatives [1] I recommended that the tax system be revised substantially as follows:

(1) By allowing a 25% reduction in the tax on earned income;

(2) By reducing the normal tax rates from 4% to 3% and from 8% to 6%;

(3) By reducing the surtax rates by commencing their application at $10,000 instead of $6,000, and scaling them progressively upwards to 25% at $100,000;

[1] (See Appendix A.)

(4) By repealing the telegraph and admission taxes and certain small miscellaneous taxes;

(5) By making certain changes in the revenue laws in the interest of simplicity and clarity, eliminating methods of tax avoidance and providing a more satisfactory method of determining tax liability.

The provision of widest general interest, because it affected everyone, was the proposed reduction of the normal tax rates. The following table shows the saving to taxpayers in the lower brackets under the rates proposed:

INCOME TAX PAYABLE UPON CERTAIN EARNED NET INCOMES

NET INCOME	SINGLE PERSON		HEAD OF FAMILY WITH DEPENDENT CHILDREN	
	Present law	Proposed	Present law	Proposed
$1,000	$0.00	$0.00	$0.00	$0.00
2,000	40.00	22.50	0.00	0.00
3,000	80.00	45.00	0.00	0.00
4,000	120.00	67.50	28.00	15.75
5,000	160.00	90.00	68.00	38.25
6,000	240.00	135.00	128.00	72.00
7,000	330.00	180.00	186.00	99.00
8,000	420.00	225.00	276.00	144.00
9,000	510.00	270.00	366.00	189.00
10,000	600.00	315.00	456.00	234.00

The Treasury actuaries estimated that under the proposed rates the Government would sustain a loss in revenue and the tax-payers a saving of about ninety-two million dollars in the brackets under $6,000, and fifty-two million dollars in the brackets from $6,000 to $10,000, or a total saving of one hundred and forty-four million dollars in the brackets under $10,000 a year. About 70% of the loss in revenue to the Government would come from the brackets under $10,000 and only 2½% of the loss in revenue would come from the brackets of income in excess of $100,000 a year. It was estimated that even this 2½% loss would be more than made up in the second year of the operation of the law.

The provision of next widest general interest was the recommendation for a reduction of 25% in the tax on earned income as compared with that paid upon incomes derived from business or investments. The fairness of taxing more lightly incomes from wages, salaries and professional services than the incomes from business or from investments is beyond question. In the first case, the income is uncertain and limited in duration; sickness or death destroys it and old age diminishes it. In the other, the source of the income continues; the income may be disposed of during a man's life and it descends to his heirs.

Surely we can afford to make a distinction between the people whose only capital is their mental and physical energy, and the people whose income is derived from investments. Such a distinction would mean much to millions of American workers and would be an added inspiration to the man who must provide a competence during his few productive years to care for himself and his family when his earning capacity is at an end.

All income under $5,000 should be considered earned income. Under such a construction, substantial justice would be done and the administration of the law would be simplified. There is, of course, absolutely no reason for placing a limitation of $20,000 or any other sum on earned income. If the distinction between unearned income and earned income is good, it is good in every bracket. One man can earn $20,000 a year just as surely as another can earn $5,000. If the tax on unearned incomes in excess of $20,000 is at the proper rate, then the same rate is too high for earned incomes.

The third outstanding feature of the Treasury's recommendations was the proposal for a revision of the surtaxes. As this was practically the only recommendation on which a very great division of opinion arose, I shall leave it for consideration in a later chapter.

Another recommendation was that the deductions for capital losses should be limited to 12½% of the loss. Capital assets may be defined as property held by the taxpayer for profit or investment for more than two years. The present revenue law limits the tax on capital gains to 12½% but puts no limit on the deductions for capital losses. I believe that it would be sounder taxation policy generally not to recognize either capital gain or capital loss for purposes of income tax. This is the policy adopted in practically all other countries having income tax laws, but it has not been the policy in the United States.

In all probability, more revenue has been lost to the Government by permitting the deduction of capital losses than has been realized by including capital gains as income. So long, however, as our law recognizes capital gains and capital losses for income tax purposes, gain and loss should be placed upon the same basis, and the provision of the 1921 Act taxing capital gains at 12½% should be extended to capital losses, so that the amount by which the tax may be reduced on account of capital loss will not exceed 12½% of the loss. It is estimated that such a provision in the law would increase the revenues by about twenty-five million dollars.

Deductions from gross income for interest

paid during the year and for losses not of a business character should be limited to the amount the sum of these items exceeds the tax-exempt income of the taxpayer. The 1921 Act provides that interest on indebtedness to acquire or carry tax-exempt securities is not deductible. This provision is ineffective because a taxpayer may purchase tax-exempt securities for cash and borrow money for other purposes. So long as a taxpayer has income which is not reached for taxation, he should not be permitted to deduct his non-business losses from the income which is taxable, but should be restricted in the first instance to a deduction of these losses on his non-taxable income. The estimated increase of revenue from this source is thirty-five million dollars.

In some States the income of the husband is the joint income of the husband and wife, and each, therefore, is permitted to file a return for one-half of the income. This gives an unfair advantage to the citizens of those States over the citizens of the other States of this country, and, to correct this inequality, it was recommended that the Federal Government tax community property income to the spouse having control of the income. It was estimated that such a provision in the law would increase the revenues by about eight million dollars.

A recommendation was also made that the tax on telegrams, telephones and leased wires should be repealed. This is the last remaining of the transportation taxes established during the war. It is a source of inconvenience to every person using the telephone or telegraph, and should now be eliminated from the tax system. The Treasury estimated that the repeal of this tax would mean a loss in revenue of about thirty million dollars a year.

Another war tax which should be repealed is the tax on admissions. The greater part of this revenue is derived from the admissions charged by neighborhood moving picture theatres. The tax is, therefore, paid by the great bulk of the people whose main source of recreation is attending the movies in the neighborhood of their homes. The loss in revenue would be about seventy million dollars, but it would constitute a direct saving to a large number of people whose tax burden should be lightened wherever it is possible to do so.

The Treasury also suggested to Congress the possibility of eliminating various small miscellaneous taxes which have an inconsiderable bearing on the general revenue of the Government and are a source of inconvenience to taxpayers as well as difficult to collect. These changes are in line with the theory that taxation should be simplified and made effective for bringing in revenue without constantly annoying and irritating the taxpayer. In carrying out this theory, it is highly important, of course, that the revenue laws should be strengthened by eliminating methods heretofore used by taxpayers to avoid payment of taxes.

Every effort should be made to simplify administration of the laws and to permit a prompt determination of liability in a manner more satisfactory to the taxpayer. As one step toward this end, the Treasury recommended the establishment of a Board of Tax Appeals in the Treasury but independent of the Bureau of Internal Revenue, to hear and determine cases involving the assessment of internal revenue taxes. The Board would sit locally in the various judicial circuits throughout the country. This would give an independent administrative tribunal equipped to hear both sides of the controversy, which would sit on appeals from the Bureau of Internal Revenue and make decisions which would be conclusive on both the Bureau and the taxpayer on the question of assessment. The taxpayer, in the event that decision should be against him, would have to pay the tax according to the assessment and have recourse to the courts, while the Government, in case decision should be against it, would likewise be obliged to have recourse to the courts, in order to enforce the collection of the tax. In a hearing in the courts, the findings of the Board should be taken as prima facie evidence of the facts contained therein.

In other nations having income tax laws, privacy of returns is respected. In every State in the United States, with one exception, privacy of returns is guaranteed by law. That exception is Wisconsin, where the privacy provision of the act has been repealed, but the validity of the law has been attacked successfully in the lower courts and final decision has not yet been received from the Supreme Court. As regards the Federal law, it would not be objectionable if the privacy of returns be removed so far as certain committees of Congress are concerned, provided that the returns are submitted to the committees only in executive session and mention of the returns on the floor of Congress and the publication thereof in the *Congressional Record* be prevented. But there can be no privacy if the returns are discussed in open committee or on the floor of Congress.

It was estimated that the recommendations for changes in the tax laws, as stated
above, would have the following effect on the
Government's revenues:

	DECREASE (in millions of dollars)	INCREASE (in millions of dollars)
Reduction of 25% in tax on earned income	97	....
Reduction in normal tax	92	....
Readjustment of surtax rates	102	....
Capital loss limited to 12½%	....	25
Interest and capital loss deductions limited	....	35
Community property amendment	....	8
Repeal of telegraph and telephone tax	30	....
Repeal of admissions tax	70	....
Total	391	68
	68	
Net Loss	323	

The benefits of the reduction will be distributed among all classes of taxpayers, and
the revision generally will help to free business and industry of vexatious interference
and encourage in all lines a more healthy
development of productive enterprise.

CHAPTER IV

SURTAXES

CHAPTER IV

SURTAXES

THE surtax is the outgrowth of war conditions. It is based on the theory that the man of large income should pay more proportionately than the smaller taxpayer. If A has twice as much income as B, then A pays not twice but three or four times as much tax. It is a progressively increasing tax, which ranges from 1% to 50%, beginning at incomes of $6,000 a year. As an example of how the surtax operates, a man with an income of $1,000,000 has the same aggregate income as 200 men each with incomes of $5,000, but the 200 small incomes pay a tax of $38.25 each or an aggregate tax of $7,650, whereas the millionaire under the Treasury's recommendations will pay a tax of $298,792. The one large income pays 40 times the tax paid by the 200 smaller incomes of equal aggregate amount, or the same amount of tax as 7,800 men with an income of $5,000 each or a total income of $39,000,000.

In addition to the surtax, of course, the same taxpayers pay the normal tax of 4% on the first $4,000 of their incomes and an additional 8% on all income in excess of that amount, so that the very large incomes are taxed as much as 58%. If A, for instance, has an income of $6,000, his tax is $240, whereas B, with an income of $12,000, is taxed $240 on the first $6,000 and $560 on the second $6,000, making a total tax of $800, or more than three times the tax levied on A.

Under the Treasury's recommendations it was proposed that the surtax should be revised, making the application of the surtax begin with incomes of $10,000 instead of $6,000, and increasing progressively upwards to 25% on all incomes of $100,000 and over. Incomes under $10,000 would pay no surtax at all; incomes over $100,000 would pay the maximum of 25%, plus the normal tax.

To the average man, it seems not unfair that the taxpayer with an income of over $200,000 a year should pay over half of it to the Government. It is a well-known fact that most people of great wealth use a comparatively small amount of their incomes for their own and their families' personal physical needs. Taxation, however, is not a means of confiscating wealth but of raising necessary revenues for the Government.

One of the foundations of our American civilization is equality of opportunity, which presupposes the right of each man to enjoy the fruits of his labor after contributing his fair share to the support of the Government, which protects him and his property. But that is a very different matter from confiscating a part of his wealth, not because the country requires it for the prosecution of a war or some other purpose, but because he seems to have more money than he needs. Our civilization, after all, is based on accumulated capital, and that capital is no less vital to our prosperity than is the extraordinary energy which has built up in this country the greatest material civilization the world has ever seen. Any policy that deliberately destroys that accumulated capital under the spur of no necessity is striking directly at the soundness of our financial structure and is full of menace for the future.

In time of war or great public necessity, unusual tax measures can always be justified. During the World War, surtaxes were evolved to meet the extraordinary commitments necessary for the successful prosecution of the war. For a time the surtax rates produced a large income, but since the close of the war, their productivity has steadily declined and the man of large income has tended more and more to invest his capital in such a way that the tax collector cannot reach it.

This is clearly shown by the statistics for the six-year period extending from 1916 to

1921. The preparation of income statistics is a matter of considerable time and labor and cannot be done until all returns from the collectors can be assembled, examined and tabulated. The statistics of 1921 returns were completed in October, 1923, and are the latest figures available. The force of these statistics, as may be seen from the table on page 74, is most compelling.

This table contains the total net incomes reported from all classes as well as the net incomes of those in the $300,000 class. For the full six-year period (1916-1921) shown in the table, it will be noticed that the total net incomes returned for taxation have increased from $6,298,000,000 to $19,577,000,-000, whereas incomes in the $300,000 class have decreased from nearly $1,000,000,000 in 1916 to $153,000,000 in 1921, and the number of taxpayers in that class has fallen from 1,296 to 246. Again referring to the same table, it will be noted that dividends and taxable interest on investments have increased during the period from $3,200,000,000 to

TABLE SHOWING DECLINE OF TAXABLE INCOMES OVER $300,000

YEAR	NUMBER OF RETURNS		NET INCOME		DIVIDENDS AND INTEREST ON INVESTMENTS	
	All classes	Incomes over $300,000	All classes	Incomes over $300,000	All classes	Incomes over $300,000
1916	437,036	1,296	$6,298,577,620	$992,972,986	$3,217,348,030	$706,945,738
1917	3,472,890	1,015	13,652,383,207	731,372,153	3,785,557,955	616,119,892
1918	4,425,114	627	15,924,639,355	401,107,868	3,872,234,935	344,111,461
1919	5,332,760	679	19,859,491,448	440,011,589	3,954,553,925	314,984,884
1920	7,259,944	395	23,735,629,183	246,354,585	4,445,145,223	229,052,039
1921	6,662,176	246	19,577,212,528	153,534,305	4,167,291,294	155,370,228

$4,160,000,000, whereas dividends and taxable interest on investments of the $300,000 class of taxpayers have decreased from $706,000,-000 to $155,000,000. The table further discloses that whereas the year 1920 shows a peak in total net incomes and total dividends and taxable interest on investments, it made no halt in the progressive diminution in the number of taxpayers with incomes in the $300,000 class, in their total net incomes, or in their incomes from dividends and taxable interest on investments.

Year	Total Surtax	Surtax on Income in Excess of $300,000	Percentage of Total of Those in Excess of $300,000
1916[1]	$121,946,136	$81,404,194	66.8
1917	433,345,732	201,937,975	46.5
1918	651,289,027	220,218,131	33.8
1919	801,525,303	243,601,410	30.4
1920	596,803,767	134,709,112	22.6
1921	411,327,684	84,797,344	20.6

[1] 1916 was a year of low surtax rates.

The above table shows the amount of surtax returned on account of incomes in excess of $300,000 for the six-year period, together with the total surtax returned and the percentage the surtax on incomes in excess of $300,000 was in relation to the total surtax.

From this it is clearly seen that, whereas the total surtax has varied, the percentage of surtax paid by the $300,000 class has progressively decreased from 66.8% to 20.6%, without a break for any prosperous year. We have, therefore, for the six years of varying degrees of prosperity, statistics showing a marked and continuous tendency.

In view of the increase in net income of the country from 1916 to 1921, as shown by the above statistics, it can hardly be contended that there were fewer men of large wealth in the country in 1916 than in 1921. The question is, therefore, where did the income of these men go, since it was not reported for taxation?

There is no doubt of the fact that much of it went into tax-exempt securities. There are over $12,000,000,000 of wholly tax-exempt securities outstanding, and the loss of revenue to the Government over what it would receive if the income were taxable is estimated at over $200,000,000 a year, and the loss of revenue over a similar investment in productive business at over $400,000,000 a year. In the 1921 Revenue Act the Congress removed the requirement that tax-exempt income be reported. The extent to which people of wealth have had resort to this means of avoidance is not available to the Government except in returns for inheritance tax purposes.

It has been contended in correspondence addressed to me that tax-exempt securities are not attractive as compared with bank stocks and industrials which yield from 10 to 100% on their investment. Such a statement, of course, is misleading if the basis is made the amount originally invested. The proper basis is the market value of the securities. The question is, can a taxpayer get more return after income taxes out of $1,000 worth of tax-exempt securities or out of

$1,000 worth of some taxable investment? I know of no sound bank stock which yields as high as 10% on what it can be sold for and the proceeds put in tax-exempt securities, nor do I know any sound investments which run up to 100% on the market value of the stock. It is true that speculation sometimes gives these high returns, but it is the very demand for such returns on account of the high surtaxes that has kept capital out of ordinary productive business and attracted it only to such projects as give opportunity for undue profit.

Standard Oil stocks in 1923 have been cited as an example of investments which would be made in preference to tax-exempt securities. This argument is most appropriately answered by the return of the estate of Mr. William Rockefeller, who was doubtless familiar with the possibilities of the Standard Oil companies. The total market value of his investments in those stocks was less than $7,000,000, whereas the value of his wholly tax-exempt bonds was over $44,000,000 or six times the amount he held in the four Standard Oil companies.

Many men of great wealth in this country have put some or all of their fortunes into tax-exempt securities. In the cases of these men, high surtaxes are becoming less and less productive of revenue; and in many cases they have become barren. It is incredible that a system of taxation which permits a man with an income of $1,000,000 a year to pay not one cent to the support of his Government should remain unaltered.

What is the remedy? It is time to face the facts and to recognize that merely levying high surtaxes will not halt the flight of capital away from taxable investments. Just as labor cannot be forced to work against its will, so it can be taken for granted that capital will not work unless the return is worth while. It will continue to retire into the shelter of tax-exempt bonds, which offer both security and immunity from the tax collector.

Congress has refused, in spite of repeated

requests by the Treasury, to submit to the States a Constitutional amendment, taking away the tax-exempt privilege now enjoyed by State, county and municipal bonds. There is consequently only one course to pursue. It must be made more profitable for wealth to go into taxable business than into tax-exempt bonds.

The Treasury has accordingly recommended that a maximum surtax of 25% plus 6% normal tax be imposed in lieu of the 58% tax now levied on the largest incomes. Such a reduction is necessary in order to attract the large fortunes back into productive enterprise.

The Treasury has been asked how this figure was determined. The question is one to which ordinary business experience must give answer. If a man is manufacturing any article of commerce, he will endeavor to fix a price for his product at a point which will yield a profit and at the same time stimulate a demand for what he has to sell. If he puts his price too low, his sales are large but his profits small; if he puts his price too high, his profit for each article is large but his sales fall off, so that his total profit again is low. Somewhere between these extremes is the price at which he will make the most money.

An income tax is the price which the Government charges for the privilege of having taxable income. If the price is too low, the Government's revenue is not large enough; if the price is too high, the taxpayer, through the many means available, avoids a taxable income and the Government gets less out of a high tax than it would out of a lower one. What the proper figure is between these extremes is not determinable with absolute accuracy. It is the opinion of some authorities on taxation that this figure is below 15%. None of them places it as high as 25%. Clearly, 58% is excessive. For example, an investor is offered a prospect of going into a business returning 11%. He also has the choice of buying a municipal bond paying 4½% which, to a man of large income, returns the same net income as the 11% business.

No business returning 11% net is as sound as a municipal bond. Consequently the investor puts his money into tax-exempt securities; the Government gets no tax and productive business is deprived of the capital.

Everyone at all active in business is acquainted with many instances where new projects have not been consummated on account of high surtaxes. With the proposed maximum rate of 6% normal tax plus 25% surtax, an investment yielding 6½% would be the equivalent of a 4½% tax-exempt bond. Businesses with reasonable assurance of such a return can be found, with the speculative probability of greater return. The investor, with the chance of making more, will go into business and reject the tax-exempt security. As a consequence, he will have a taxable income in which the Government will share instead of income yielding no revenue whatever to the Government.

An interesting illustration of this is the situation in 1916, when, with surtax rates running up to 13% as a maximum, the Government collected from the $300,000 class $81,000,000 in surtaxes. In 1921, with the surtax reaching 65%, the Government collected from the same class of taxpayers $84,000,000. In other words, the Government received substantially the same revenue from high incomes with a 13% surtax as it received with a 65% surtax. It is not too much to hope that some day we may get back on a tax basis of 10%, the old Hebrew tithe, which was always considered a fairly heavy tax.

The analysis which the Treasury has made of the tax situation, as well as the remedy which it has proposed, has received the support of one of the most eminent authorities on taxation in the country. The following extract is quoted from an open letter to the Chairman of the Committee on Ways and Means of the House of Representatives written by Thomas S. Adams, Professor of Economics at Yale University, former President of the National Tax Association, formerly a member of the Wisconsin State Board of Tax Commissioners, and Tax Adviser to the

United States Treasury Department from 1917 to 1921. After reviewing the question of tax avoidance under the present law and recognizing the impossibility of immediately closing all the holes in the law, by means of which tax payment is avoided, he makes the following statement with reference to the revision of the surtaxes:

"Assuming that the holes in the income tax will not be closed in the near future, what conclusions fairly follow with respect to the upper surtaxes?

"I shall not insult your intelligence by asserting that there is a precise maximum surtax, definitely known or demonstrable, which inevitably 'follows as the day the night' from the above premise. It is possible, for instance, that a few inexperienced members of Congress may not know of the ease with which the income tax may be legally avoided, when high rates provide a sufficient incentive. Again, there may be a few idealistic congressmen who so fervently believe that the rich ought to pay 40 to 50 per cent of their incomes, that they would rather assert this obligation in the tax law and not collect the tax, than vote for a 25 per cent rate, or any other rate which can be collected.

"But the practical and experienced congressman, if I understand his position, does not wish to be placed in these groups nor be judged by the standards applicable to such groups. He is after results and elects to be judged by the actual fruits of the legislation which he supports. Surely such a congressman, if the holes in the tax remain open, and he nevertheless votes for surtaxes of 38 or 40 per cent, cannot go to his constituents and conscientiously say: 'I have voted to make the rich pay what they ought to pay.' The most that he can fairly say is: 'I have voted for the rates which the rich ought to pay, and hope within the next four or five years to find ways and means of closing the holes by which most rich men now avoid such rates.'

"The latter, I gather, is the position of those who, knowing that the holes are open, nevertheless vote for the rates that make the rich utilize these holes. They propose 'to narrow some of these holes at this session of Congress and close more of them in the future.' I do not sneer at this position. It is one that an honest and intelligent man could conceivably take. But it overlooks and forgets one crucial fact. It assumes that, four or five years from now, when we get around to the task of patching up the holes in the income tax, we shall have the kind of income tax that can be patched up. *The probability is strong that in four or five years the income tax will, as a matter of practical politics, be past patching.*

* * * * * *

"We debate and dispute about the minutiæ of rates, when the question is the honesty or integrity—and hence the real life—of the progressive income tax.

"The income tax will not be saved by lifting from its load a mere straw. Reducing the maximum surtax from 50 to 44, or even to 40 per cent, would in my opinion be useless. It would be cutting off the tail by inches. Taxpayers who will avoid 50 per cent surtaxes, will avoid 40 per cent and, in my deliberate judgment, 35 per cent surtaxes. There are some occasions when a half loaf is better than nothing at all. This is not one of those occasions. I can see no justification in principle for a cut in the maximum surtax of 10 or 12 per cent. There should be greater reduction or no reduction at all. The reason or justification for cutting the upper surtaxes is not to reduce the taxes of the few rich men who happen to be caught. The justification is to get a tax that can be enforced; to reduce the discrepancy between the taxation of corporations and the taxation of individuals; to give back to certain lines of business whose normal supply of credit comes from wealthy individuals, their normal and natural investment market; and most of all, to give to the income tax at this critical period a task which it can creditably perform.

"When revenue is needed, most Americans (including myself) believe in levying the highest progressive rates that can be imposed without doing more harm than good to the nation as a whole. But at this moment, any rate is too high that will retard the restoration of the income tax to health and working efficiency. Any rate is too high that pushes the income tax into deeper disrepute. With the holes in the income tax wide open, it seems to me that its friends should be the first to resent and oppose rates which expose the tax to contempt as a complicated nightmare of political dreamers. We want an effective progressive tax, not a gesture.

"If the new income tax—the income tax of 1924—fails to reach and actually tax the richer taxpayers, whose fault will it be? Who will be responsible for the further degradation of the income tax?

"We shall not be able to blame the rich. They escape, for the most part, by legal avoidance, not by illegal evasion. Few people, rich or poor, pay taxes which they can lawfully avoid.

"We shall not be able to blame the administration, if the tax law carries rates which Secretary Mellon and his Democratic predecessors have said it is impossible to collect in times of peace. Secretary Mellon will have a perfect alibi.

"But he has stated as his opinion that a maximum surtax of 25 per cent will reverse the tide of avoidance and permit the income tax to be creditably, if not perfectly, administered. Under such circumstances, is it not the wisest thing for those who genuinely care for the future welfare of the income tax to take Secretary Mellon at his word? Give him the 25 per cent maximum which he requests, and then hold him and his administration responsible for results.

"In the name of political honesty, what difference does it make whether the maximum tax be 65 per cent, 45 per cent, or 35 per cent, if such rates will not be collected in a dwindling minority of cases?"

CHAPTER V

TAXING ENERGY AND INITIATIVE

Chapter V

Taxing Energy and Initiative

If high surtaxes were becoming merely ineffective we might let the system stand until the Government should be obliged to seek other sources of revenue. But a much more serious matter is involved. The flight of capital into safe but unproductive forms of investment should give us great concern, for it indicates that high surtaxes are gradually destroying business initiative.

The existing system of taxation was framed to meet war-time conditions. But with the passing of those conditions and the continuance of the unscientific tax rates, the burden is now being borne chiefly by the man of initiative attempting to make money under the usual conditions of business competition. These rates bear most heavily on the producer, the salaried man and those engaged in trying to make a competence for their later, unproductive years. They penalize principally the middle incomes, while permitting wealth to escape by investment in tax-exempt securities and by other available methods. The vital defect in our present system is that the tax burden is borne by wealth in the making, not by capital already in existence. We place a tax on energy and initiative; and at the same time provide a refuge in the form of tax-exempt securities, into which wealth that has been accumulated or inherited can retire and defy the tax collector. We have under the high surtaxes a system that increases the actual tax burden on the men of moderate incomes and allows many of the largest incomes to escape taxation.

Initiative has always been the most valuable American characteristic. It was this spirit in the early colonists which brought them to America, not to find an easier existence, but to enjoy religious and political freedom, as well as to better their material condition. They faced death by savages and starvation in order to build up a new country. It was the same spirit of adventure which peopled and developed the West. And it is this same spirit extended into business that has made America the great and prosperous nation she is today.

The United States is no mere happy accident. What we have has been achieved by courage and hard work. The spirit of business adventure has built up in this country a civilization which offers unprecedented rewards to any man who is willing to work. But where the Government takes away an unreasonable share of his earnings, the incentive to work is no longer there and a slackening of effort is the result. To share not at all in a man's losses and to take one-half of his gains, making him work three days out of six for the Government, is to impose odds too heavy to be borne. More and more the business adventure becomes too hazardous and the high spirit of initiative disappears in discouragement. An economic system which permits wealth in existence to escape its share in the expense of the Government, and wealth in creation to be penalized until the creative spirit is destroyed, cannot be the right system for America.

Henry Ford is one of the outstanding examples of what American initiative has accomplished in the last twenty years. Under the conditions which then obtained in this country, he has built up one of the great industrial establishments of the world, giving employment to thousands and adding to the comfort of millions of individuals by placing within their reach an automobile of moderate cost. In a recent interview he told why such an accomplishment would have been impossible under the present high surtaxes.

Starting out with a small capital, he put his profits back into the business and these in turn were used to buy better machinery, thus making it possible to reduce the price of his cars. If the present tax rates had been in force, most of these profits would have been paid to the Government and Mr. Ford doubts that it would have been possible ever to reach a point where he could have produced a car under $1500. Mr. Ford added:

"High taxes on the rich do not take burdens off the poor. They put burdens on the poor. As far as our company is concerned, we can go on about as we now are, whether the surtax be 25% or 50%. We can make some improvements, but we cannot do the great things we should do had we more money. We cannot make such progress in the next fifteen years as we have in the last fifteen, and all other forward-looking companies will be in exactly the same boat."

Mr. Richard Olney, formerly a member of Congress and now engaged in the wool business in Boston, had the following to say about the surtaxes:

"As a member of a firm of wool merchants, we have a customer operating about ten sets of woolen machinery, who, about a year ago, made plans to enlarge his plant fully one-half to meet an increasing demand for manufactured goods, but, consulting with his partners, he decided on account of the high surtaxes to invest the surplus balance in profits from the firm in non-taxable securities. In other words, he resented the penalty imposed by the Government upon thrift through a severely high surtax and invested his surplus balance in profits where he would receive a fair income involving no great risk and anxiety.''

Another interesting bit of testimony in connection with still another great industry was contained in a letter received by the Treasury from Mr. Daniel Guggenheim. Mr. Guggenheim said:

"Up to a few years ago our operations were upon a progressively increasing scale; at the present time they are upon a greatly reduced scale, and the reason is because of the unduly high surtaxes upon incomes. The net result is a great decline in our ability to do that which we would like to do in the promotion of American enterprise, business activity and prosperity.

"Until recent years it was not uncommon for us directly through our firm or through corporations created for that purpose, to spend fully $500,000 each year in the mere examination of mining properties. Today our expenses in that direction are practically nil, and the large organization which we had built up, for that purpose, has been virtually dissolved.

"Under the present plan of taxation, the business man must assume the burden of all losses, whereas the Government through taxes takes so large a share of the profits that in a business such as mining, involving great risks of loss, the possible net return—under existing law— does not warrant taking the chances involved.

"If a reduction in the surtaxes is made in accordance with your proposals, there is no doubt that I will personally be relieved from certain taxation. But that fact will not add to my personal comfort or expenditure; it will merely enable me to make a further investment in profitable enterprise, the profits from which will in turn be subject to taxation. A change in the plan of taxation, under which those who earn substantial profits may retain a sufficient share of them to compensate for possible losses, will very decidedly affect the vigor of not alone our own but all American business effort.''

One of the most interesting letters received by the Treasury was written to a senator by a woman engaged in the dressmaking business. The following extract is quoted from the letter:

"This is a woman's endorsement of Secretary Mellon's plan for reducing Federal taxes, and I want to give you my reasons as briefly as possible.

"For ten years I have been engaged in the business of designing, making and selling embroidered dresses and dress patterns.

"This business gives employment to several hundred women in Kentucky and in other States. Aside from the executive and clerical staff, workers are employed as designers, as embroiderers and some as canvassers.

"They are thus enabled to live in their own homes—largely in the country districts, to develop their special talents in congenial and profitable employment, to supplement the family income, and in many instances to support and educate their families and to lay aside something for a rainy day.

"The success of this business is a vital thing for these employes—quite as much so as for me. Its success depends, of course, upon ourselves, but also upon our ability to sell our dresses.

"Ability to sell depends upon ability of our customers to buy, and this, in turn, upon their chance to reduce expenses and effect those small economies by which women save in order that they may secure for themselves the things that beautify and brighten life.

"Now the object of this letter is simply to put our story before you—to tell you of the great burden upon our business. This burden comes, not merely in direct taxes, but even more in limiting the purchasing powers of *those who would buy* from us *if they could,* but who cannot buy if they in turn are stripped by taxation.

"Thus industry lags and our own workers lack employment and hands are idle whose deft fingers might make beautiful things that capable women in turn could sell if only customers *could buy*.

"I cannot estimate this direct loss of business, due to the burdens of taxation, nor can I appraise the evils accruing to the Government itself from piling up taxes that are more than its necessary expenses. An obvious result is a demand for a distribution of such accumulation. There will always be classes in the community insisting that the Government owes them something. Few of them will profit by any donation that may be made by the Government, which, after all, takes from the producing class what it gives in so-called bounty.

"I am a woman. My business associates are women. We have built up our business from nothing, without special benefits from legislation or taxation. We do not want any, but we do want a chance to make our own way unhampered by excessive tax burdens.

"For the years 1919, 1920 and 1921, the annual burden of Federal taxes upon our combined efforts was an average of 42 per cent of the net income of our business. Our customers felt the pinch of taxation in the same way, if not to the same extent.

"As a result, in 1922 we had no profits, and the government no taxes from our business. It is the old story of killing the goose that laid golden eggs.

"I am sure that, if you could see this subject through the eyes of women in business, you would realize the *absolute necessity of giving some relief.*"

These letters give convincing testimony of the effect of the high surtaxes upon four important, unrelated industries. Similar testimony could be cited of other trades and industries affected in like manner.

The flow of capital into tax-exempt securities has been felt particularly in two other businesses of great importance to the general public. It is estimated that the railroads will require a billion dollars a year of new capital in order satisfactorily to provide the facilities and equipment requisite to handle the traffic presented and to reduce the cost of transportation. In earlier years the railroads have been able to maintain a reasonable proportion between their total stock issues and their total interest obligations. As illustrative of this, the percentages of new bond issues to new stock issues in the three years 1911, 1912, 1913, were respectively 59 per cent, 60 per cent, and 53 per cent. In the last three years, under high surtaxes, these percentages have become 100 per cent, 95 per cent, and 94 per cent. The time is rapidly approaching when the railroads will be unable to issue further bonds without substantial increase in the stock investment. Originally railroad stocks have been purchased and held by wealthy men and the bonds have more generally gone into the hands of the smaller investor. The Supreme Court has recently sustained the validity of the "recapture clause," which effectually prevents any new stock being sold at a price which would give a man with large income an adequate return on his investment. If the railroads are to be furnished with capital, much of it must come from the sale of stock and to permit any sale surtaxes must be so reduced as to attract the large investor to that type of security. Under the present surtaxes a 6% stock nets a man of small income 6%. It nets the man of large wealth but 3%. The correction of this situation obviously lies in a lowering of surtaxes.

There is still an acute shortage of housing facilities in the large cities of this country. While it is true that the high cost of material and labor has contributed to this shortage, the real reason why capital has not been more attracted to this investment is the surtaxes. If a flat building could be built in 1913 on a $100,000 investment, and the investor desired 8 per cent return, his rents had to be adjusted so as to give him net $8,000. If in 1923 a similar building should require $200,000, the investor, to get the same return after high surtaxes, would need net rents of $38,000. He would probably, however, wish to provide against this abnormal cost of building by amortizing the excess cost and demand net rents of $48,000.

We have either the failure to make investment because of the unlikelihood of adequate return, or a gouging of the tenants.

It does not change the situation if the building operation is done through a corporation. The individual investor in the corporation is interested in what he receives. The interposition of a corporate entity between the rents of the tenant and the profits to the investor, taking into account the capital stock tax of the corporation, means substantially the same outgo for taxes to the Government. Rents must be even higher than in the case of individual investors.

It would seem necessary to reduce the surtaxes, not only as a means of saving the productivity of the system, but also on account of the far-reaching effect which such a reduction would have on the country's continued development. It is a strange theory of taxation which, in order to make the gesture of taxing the rich, retains rates that are producing less and less revenue each year and at the same time discouraging industry and threatening the country's future prosperity. It is true that many existing industries are prospering and that the country's condition today is sound. But new investments are not being made in sufficient number and new enterprises are starting out under a disadvantage as compared with old established ones. No useful purpose will be served by pretending to reduce the surtaxes. In order to have any economic effect at all, they must be cut far enough to free capital for new enterprises. In other words, we must return again to an economically sound basis of taxation.

CHAPTER VI

ESTATE TAXES

CHAPTER VI

ESTATE TAXES

A DISPOSITION has been manifested recently in Congress to increase inheritance taxes from the present maximum of 25% to a maximum of 40%. Such legislation would be most unwise from every point of view.

In the first place, the right of the Federal Government to tax inheritances is based upon no specific Constitutional power, but upon the theory of an excise tax. These taxes have been used heretofore only to obtain additional revenue in time of war and should be preserved for such use in the future.

They have been levied four times in the country's history, and may be known as the Revolutionary War Tax, enacted in 1797 and repealed in 1802; the Civil War Tax, enacted in 1862 and repealed in 1870; the

111

Spanish War Tax, which remained on the statute books from 1898 to 1902; and the present Inheritance Tax, which was enacted in 1916 and subsequently amended. The rates now reach a maximum of 25% in addition to the heavy estate taxes imposed by the various States in which the decedents' property is located. While the States should do their share in the reduction of these taxes, the Federal tax is very heavy and should be lightened, not increased, if the ultimate good of the country is to be taken into consideration.

Inheritance taxes are properly sources of revenue for the States. They are a material element in a State budget; they are a comparatively small element in the Federal budget. The whole return which the Federal Government receives from estate taxes, amounting to about $110,000,000 under present rates, is insignificant in comparison with the general receipts of the Government. To deprive the States of this source of revenue, properly their own, is to compel them to increase taxes and to resort still further to their principal source of income, which consists in levies on land.

It is difficult to understand the attitude of a man who opposes the adoption of a Constitutional amendment taking away the tax-exempt privilege of State and municipal securities because he feels it would be an invasion of "States rights," and yet advocates the permanent levy by the Federal Government of higher and higher estate taxes, which are essentially taxes to be levied by the States, rather than the Federal Government. In advocating lower estate taxes and a restriction of tax-exempt securities, the Treasury has been actuated in both cases by a desire to save the productivity of the revenues, which is seriously threatened under the existing system of taxation. In the case of tax-exempt securities, the States would give up no right by the adoption of the amendment but would merely cease to profit at the expense of the Federal Government. In the case of estate taxes, on the other hand, the

States have certain definite rights which should never be invaded by the Federal Government, except in times of great necessity, as, for instance, in the conduct of wars.

The character of taxation should not be such as to destroy the very source from which revenue is to flow. Almost every State in the Union has an estate or inheritance tax, and every estate pays, therefore, not only the Federal tax but the tax of the State of the residence of the decedent, plus, under the present modern system of investment, the taxes of one or more other States. The total tax—always two taxes and often three or four, may take more than half of a large estate, and cases are possible where it would take practically the entire property. The situation here is even worse than in England, where there is but one tax. Here there are several.

The table on page 115 shows at a glance the estate, inheritance or legacy taxes imposed by the various States in addition to the estate taxes imposed by the Federal Government.

States	Exemption	Rates %
Alabama	. . . .	None
Alaska	$100–$10,000 . .	1–17½
Arizona	100– 10,000 . .	1–25
Arkansas	500– 3,000[1] . .	1–40
California	500– 24,000 . .	1–20
Colorado	0– 20,000 . .	0–16
Connecticut	500– 10,000 . .	1– 8
Delaware	0– 3,000 . .	1– 8
District of Columbia . . .	. . . .	None
Florida	. . . .	None
Georgia	0– 5,000 . .	1–21
Hawaii	500– 5,000 . .	0–10
Idaho	500– 10,000[2] . .	1–15
Illinois	100– 20,000 . .	2–30
Indiana	100– 15,000 . .	1–20
Iowa	0– 15,000[3] . .	0–20
Kansas	0– 75,000 . .	½–15
Kentucky	500– 10,000 . .	1–15
Louisiana	500– 5,000 . .	0–10
Maine	500– 10,000 . .	1– 7
Maryland	0–whole estate .	5
Massachusetts	1,000– 10,000 . .	1–12
Michigan	100– 5,000[4] . .	1–25
Minnesota	100– 10,000 . .	1–20
Mississippi . . . Estate . .	5,000	½
" Individual bene-		
ficiary	500– 7,500 . .	½– 8
Missouri	0– 20,000[5] . .	1–30
Montana	0– 17,500 . .	1–16
Nebraska	0– 10,000 . .	1– 6
Nevada	0– 20,000 . .	1–25
New Hampshire	0– 10,000 . .	2–10
New Jersey	0– 5,000 . .	1– 8
New Mexico	0– 10,000 . .	1– 5
New York	0– 5,000 . .	1– 8
North Carolina	0– 10,000 . .	1– 9
North Dakota	0– 10,000 . .	1–20
Ohio	0– 5,000[6] . .	1–10
Oklahoma	500– 15,000 . .	1–10
Oregon . . . Estate . . .	10,000	1–10
" Individual beneficiary	0– 1,000 . .	0–25
Pennsylvania	0	2–10
Philippine Islands	pesos 0– 3,000 . .	1–64
Porto Rico	$200– $5,000 . .	1–12

STATES		EXEMPTION	RATES %
Rhode Island . . Estate .		5,000	. . . ½–2½
" " Individual			
beneficiary		1,000– 25,000	. . ½– 8
South Carolina		200– 10,000	. . 1–14
South Dakota		100– 10,000	. . 1–20
Tennessee		1,000– 10,000	. . 1–10
Texas		500– 25,000	. . 0–20
Utah		10,000	. . 3– 5
Vermont		0– 10,000	. . 1– 5
Virginia		1,000– 10,000	. . 1–15
Washington		0– 10,000	. . 1–40
West Virginia		0– 15,000	. . 2–35
Wisconsin		100– 15,000	. . 2–40
Wyoming		1,000– 10,000	. . 0–10

[1] Plus $5,000 of value of dower or curtesy.
[2] Plus half the community property.
[3] Plus distributive share of surviving spouse.
[4] Plus an exemption of real property.
[5] Plus marital rights.
[6] Plus a widow's and children's award.

As the above table shows, all the States and territories, except three, have recourse to estate taxes, with the result that estates are taxed not alone by the Federal Government but by one or more of the States also. The time has arrived when some action to establish apportionment of taxing resources and co-ordination of their application as between the States and the Federal Government is vitally necessary.

When a man dies, his property does not often consist of cash or readily marketable securities. The estate taxes must be met in cash and not in kind. His executors must proceed to realize this cash through sales of the decedent's property. The effect of a man's death is immediately to give notice to all possible purchasers that a forced sale will soon take place. This has the effect of dropping the price at which securities can be sold and results in bringing down not only the value of such property and securities but values everywhere. The ultimate effect of this is to bring down the very values upon which the tax is levied and ultimately to destroy the productivity of the tax both to the State and to the Federal Government.

These high rates of tax in their application do not show, therefore, the true proportion of the estate taken. In its practical effect, a 40 per cent rate requires for its satisfaction 50 per cent or more of the normal value of the estate; and in cases where an estate is burdened with considerable indebtedness, as is usual where the decedent was engaged in active business, the destructive effect is still greater. Even upon investments which are of the most liquid and marketable character, the effect is to an extent the same, since the public knows that a sale must take place and there is an immediate reaction in quoted market values in anticipation of the liquidation.

Now values generally are built up and maintained by operation of the credit system. To say that a market value of a particular stock is $100 per share means only that, if some one is willing to buy the stock and some one else is willing to sell, a reasonable number of shares will change hands under these conditions at $100 per share. On the other hand, if a seller is forced to dispose of his stock, he must find a purchaser where he can and at a price at which the purchaser will buy, which is often much less than its real value. Particularly is this true where the sales have to be made in large blocks or where the company whose stock is offered is not generally known to the public. One very wealthy man in England has made a fortune almost entirely out of taking advantage of this necessity of executors.

If there were but a single instance of such forced sales, the effect on the country as a whole perhaps would not be material. When you consider, however, that death brings into the market in every decade a large proportion of the total wealth of the country, the cumulative effect upon prices is very serious. The delicate credit structure upon which these prices rest is broken down and to that extent values which we call wealth disappear. They are not transferred; they disintegrate. The wealth is gone. No tax can be more illogical than that which is destructive of the very values upon which the tax is based.

There is a point in the application of rate of tax beyond which it is impossible to extract revenue and carried to this extreme the consequences are revolutionary. For instance, assuming that all inheritances, large and small, were taxed at 40 per cent, it would then be only two or three generations until private ownership of property would cease to exist. Since these taxes are used in the current operation of the Government, the result would be not that the Government had absorbed the wealth of the country, but that the wealth had been spent and none was left.

Development of the credit structure and increase in values make the high standard of living in this country and the breaking down of these values must necessarily reduce this standard of living for everyone. A striking illustration of this truth is the case of Russia. Russia is a country of large natural resources and had great wealth. There were comprehensive commercial operations, great industrial productivity, and financial institutions with large resources in all the centers of population. The banks held commercial paper, mortgages and other instruments of credit based on land and varied production. The revolutionists contemplated the seizure of this property. They could see these values indicating the wealth which they thought they might take over. What happened? When they commenced to make destructive tax levies and seize hold of the assets of the institutions, values disappeared and almost all wealth with them. No one got it. It simply became non-existent, and all that was obtained by those who had expected to benefit in the acquisition of this wealth was the physical gold and jewels, which had no value in Russia but could be exported and sold in countries where values had not yet been destroyed. When these physical things had been disposed of, wealth entirely disappeared. Any estate tax in that country would be a dry source of revenue.

In degree England shows a similar tendency. Since it became a nation, in England land had represented wealth. By this is not meant simply unproductive residences, but land with its accompanying tenant population. Under the high death duties, ownership in land has ceased to have value and large estates can now be purchased for less than the cost of the improvements. In other words, the land itself is rendered valueless by the death duties and no longer produces revenue.

The far-reaching economic effect of high

inheritance taxes is not properly understood. These taxes are a levy upon capital. There is no requirement in our law, as there is in the English law, that the proceeds from estate taxes shall go into capital improvements of the Government. In other words, capital is being destroyed for current operating expenses and the cumulative effect of such destruction cannot fail to be harmful to the country. Estate taxes, carried to an excess, in no way differ from the methods of the revolutionists in Russia. Yet many responsible statesmen in this country, for the sake of increasing revenues by a comparatively small amount, would raise the inheritance tax rates and commit this country to a policy of confiscation of wealth.

As regards a tax on gifts, this tax also is a tax on capital, the proceeds of which do not go into capital and, therefore, work a destruction of the total capital of the country. Any annual tax on gifts is susceptible of evasion by spreading the gifts over a period of years. Such a tax will mean practically nothing by way of revenue to the Government and will be extremely difficult to detect and enforce. It has a most peculiar incidence, unlike any other tax that I know of—the one who gives pays the tax, and not the one who receives.

In considering a revision of estate taxes, there should be eliminated any question of levying the tax as a means of punishing wealth or as in some way for the social good of our civilization. The theory upon which this country was founded is equality of opportunity. So long as a man uses his abilities within the bounds of the moral sense of the community, monetary success is not a crime, but on the contrary adds to the total wealth of the country and to an increase in the standard of living as a whole.

The social necessity for breaking up large fortunes in this country does not exist. Very wisely our forefathers declined to implant in this country the principle of primogeniture under which the eldest son alone inherited and kept the properties intact. Under our American law, it is customary for estates to be divided equally among the children; and in a few generations any single large fortune is split into many moderate inheritances. As a usual thing, the continuation of a single fortune through several generations has been proven to be impossible. It is an often quoted saying that "there are three generations from shirt sleeves to shirt sleeves."

To recapitulate: the estate tax furnishes but a slight portion of the revenues to the Federal Government but it supplies a large and important part of the State revenues. To destroy values from which the States receive income is to force them to resort to higher taxes on land. The Federal Government should keep estate taxes as a reserve in times of national stress. All prior inheritance taxes have been war taxes; and it is only now that it is proposed to destroy this reserve in times when revenues from other sources are adequate and even in excess of the Nation's needs. Such a course of action is not only thoroughly unsound but borders on economic suicide.

CHAPTER VII

BENEFITS OF TAX REDUCTION

CHAPTER VII

BENEFITS OF TAX REDUCTION

TAX revision should be viewed only from the angle of what is best for the country as a whole. Taxes affect the entire country and there is no reason why their revision should ever be made a question of partisan politics.

The only controversial phase of the question is the revision of the surtaxes and, while there may be a difference of opinion as between individuals, there can be no partisan line-up on this question. Every Treasury administration, Republican and Democratic, for several years back has recommended that the surtax rates be reduced. In every case, recommendation has been based on the fact, which by this time is a matter of common knowledge, that the higher rates of surtax are not productive and in many ways actually operate to the prejudice of the revenues by encouraging investment in tax-exempt securities, in order to avoid the realization of taxable income. As long ago as 1919, Secretary of the Treasury Glass stated in his annual report:

"The upmost brackets of the surtax have already passed the point of productivity and the only consequence of any further increase would be to drive possessors of these great incomes more and more to place their wealth in the billions of dollars of wholly exempt securities heretofore issued and still being issued by States and municipalities, as well as those heretofore issued by the United States. This process not only destroys a source of revenue to the Federal Government, but tends to withdraw the capital of very rich men from the development of new enterprises and place it at the disposal of State and municipal governments upon terms so easy to them (the cost of exemptions from taxation falling more heavily upon the Federal

Government) as to stimulate wasteful and non-productive expenditure by State and municipal governments.''

At the same time President Wilson in his Message to Congress stated as follows:

"The Congress might well consider whether the higher rates of income and profits taxes can in peace times be effectively productive of revenue, and whether they may not, on the contrary, be destructive of business activity and productive of waste and inefficiency. There is a point at which in peace times high rates of income and profits taxes discourage energy, remove the incentive to new enterprise, encourage extravagant expenditures and produce industrial stagnation with consequent unemployment and other attendant evils.''

A year later Secretary of the Treasury Houston, in his annual report for the year 1920, made even more specific recommendations about the surtaxes, stating the case in the following terms:

"Since the adoption of the heavy war surtaxes in the revenue act of 1917, the Treasury has repeatedly called attention to the fact that these surtaxes are excessive; that they have passed the point of maximum productivity and are rapidly driving the wealthier taxpayers to transfer their investments into the thousands of millions of tax-free securities which compete so disastrously with the industrial and railroad securities upon the ready purchase of which the development of industry and the expansion of foreign trade intimately depend.

"It seems idle to speculate in the abstract as to whether or not a progressive income-tax schedule rising to rates in excess of 70 per cent is justifiable. We are confronted with a condition, not a theory. The fact is that such rates cannot be successfully collected. Tax returns and statistics are demonstrating what it should require no statistical evidence to prove. For the year 1916 net income amounting to $992,972,985 was included in the returns of taxpayers having net income over $300,000 a year. This aggregate fell to $731,372,153 for the year 1917 and to $392,247,329 for the year 1918. There is little reason to believe that the actual income of the richer taxpayers of the country had fallen in that interval. It is the taxable income which has been reduced and almost certainly through investment by the richer taxpayers in tax-exempt properties. Whatever one may believe, therefore, about the abstract propriety of projecting income-tax rates to a point above 70 per cent, when the taxpayers affected are subject also to State and local taxation, the fact remains that to retain such rates in the tax law is to cling to a shadow while relinquishing the substance. The effective way to tax the rich is to adopt rates that do not force investment in tax-exempt securities.''

In advocating a revision of the taxes, the Treasury has tried to secure a dispassionate consideration of the whole subject by those men in both parties who are best fitted by training and experience to give the country a sound tax system. The Under Secretary of the Treasury, Mr. Garrard B. Winston, publicly stated the position of the Treasury in a speech at Chicago, in which he said:

"There is no reason why the subject of taxation cannot be approached from a purely non-partisan viewpoint. The outstanding feature of the Mellon plan is the Secretary's recommendation for a reduction of the high surtaxes. Similar recommendations have been made by the last two preceding Secretaries of the Treasury, both of whom held their offices under a Democratic President. There is nothing political in recommending a sound basis of taxation. It is simply common sense."

President Coolidge, in his Lincoln Day address at New York on February 12, 1924 (see Appendix E), gave a masterly analysis of the tax situation and urged that the existing system be revised along the lines recommended by the Treasury. The President said:

"The first object of taxation is to secure revenue. When the taxation of large incomes is approached with that in view, the problem is to find a rate which will produce the largest returns. Experience does not show that the higher rate produces the larger revenue. Experience is all in the other way. . . .

"I agree perfectly with those who wish to relieve the small taxpayer by getting the largest possible contribution from the people with large incomes. But if the rates on large incomes are so high that they disappear, the small taxpayer will be left to bear the entire burden. If, on the other hand, the rates are placed where they will produce the most revenue from large incomes, then the small taxpayer will be relieved. The experience of the Treasury Department and the opinion of the best experts place the rate which will collect most from the people of great wealth, thus giving the largest relief to people of moderate wealth, at not over 25 per cent.

"A very important social and economic question is also involved in high rates. That is the result taxation has upon national development. Our progress in that direction depends upon two factors—personal ability and surplus income. An expanding prosperity requires that the largest possible amount of surplus income should be invested in productive enterprise under the direction of the best personal ability. This will not be done if the rewards of such action are very largely taken away by taxation. If we had a tax whereby on the first working day the Government took 5 per cent of your wages, on the second day 10 per cent, on the third day 20 per cent, on the fourth day 30 per cent, on the fifth day 50 per cent, and on the sixth day 60 per cent, how many of you would continue to work on the last two days of the week? It is the same with capital. Surplus income will go into tax-exempt securities. It will refuse to take the risk incidental to embarking in business. This will raise the rate which established business will have to pay for new capital, and result in a marked increase in the cost of living. If new capital will not flow into competing enterprise the present concerns tend toward monopoly, increasing again the prices which the people must pay. . . .

"Taken altogether, I think it is easy enough to see that I wish to include in

the program a reduction in the high surtax rates, not that small incomes may be
required to pay more and large incomes
be required to pay less, but that more
revenue may be secured from large incomes and taxes on small incomes may be
reduced; not because I wish to relieve the
wealthy, but because I wish to relieve the
country.''

A sound revision of taxes should aid ma-
terially in reducing the cost of living. High
taxes have always meant a high price level,
for the taxes are paid, in a large measure,
by consumers all over the country and not
alone by persons actually giving their checks
to the Government. No thoughtful person
longer doubts that, irrespective of his income,
he pays a part of the high surtaxes in the
general high price level.

The public should clearly understand what
is involved in the effort to re-establish in
this country a sound basis of taxation. The
question is not whether two or three million
voters shall save $10 apiece in their direct
payments of taxes or $15 apiece, but whether,

by the re-establishment of an economically sound basis of taxation, the 110,000,000 people in this country shall save much more than $10 or $15 apiece in what they pay for the necessities of life.

In addition to insisting upon a reduction of the normal rates and a reduction of the rates on earned income, the high surtax rates must be reduced to a point where capital is freed from the killing effect of these rates upon new investments. In many discussions of the tax question the present tax rates, aggregating a maximum of 58%, are treated as if they were normal rates of taxation. Any reduction from them, it is argued, is a great concession to the rich. This is not true. Before the war required the taking of every cent which could be obtained for the support of the Government in its emergency, a surtax rate reaching 13% on a two million dollar income was considered high. As was pointed out in a previous chapter, it is interesting to note that substantially as much revenue was realized from incomes over $300,000 under

CHAPTER VIII

TAX-EXEMPT SECURITIES

In a letter dated April 30, 1921, to the Chairman of the Committee on Ways and Means of the House of Representatives, I said:

"I suggest for the consideration of Congress that it may also be advisable to take action by statute or by Constitutional amendment, where necessary, to restrict further issues of tax-exempt securities. It is now the policy of the Federal Government not to issue its own obligations with exemptions from Federal surtaxes and profits taxes, but States and municipalities are issuing fully tax-exempt securities in great volume. It is estimated that there are outstanding, perhaps, ten billion dollars of fully tax-exempt securities. The existence of this mass of exempt securities constitutes an economic evil of the first magnitude. The continued issue of tax-exempt securities encourages the growth of public indebtedness and tends to divert capital from productive enterprise. Even though the exemptions of outstanding securities cannot be disturbed, it is important that future issues be controlled or prohibited by mutual consent of the State and Federal Governments.''

Subsequently, the following resolution was introduced in the House of Representatives:

(H. J. Res. 314, 67th Congress, 4th Session)

JOINT RESOLUTION Proposing an amendment to the Constitution of the United States.

Resolved by the Senate and House of Representatives of the United States of America in Congress assembled (two-thirds of each House concurring therein), That the following article is proposed as an amendment to the Constitution of the United States, which shall be valid to all intents and purposes as part of the Constitution when ratified by the legislatures of three-fourths of the several States:

"Article —.

"Section 1. The United States shall have power to lay and collect taxes on income derived from securities issued, after the ratification of this article, by or under the authority of any State, but without discrimination against income derived from such securities and in favor of income derived from securities issued, after the ratification of this article, by or under the authority of the United States or any other State.

"Sec. 2. Each State shall have power to lay and collect taxes on income derived by its residents from securities issued, after the ratification of this article, by or under the authority of the United States; but without discrimination against income derived from such securities and in favor of income derived from securities issued, after the ratification of this article, by or under the authority of such State."

This resolution passed the House of Representatives on January 23, 1923, but failed of passage in the Senate. It was reintroduced in identical words in the succeeding Congress as H. J. Res. 136, 68th Congress, 1st Session; and on February 8, 1924, failed to pass the House of Representatives, thus bringing to a close, for the present, the effort to restrict by Constitutional amendment further issues of tax-exempt securities.

The situation with regard to tax-exempt securities presents a serious problem to the country. The Treasury has estimated that the amount of such securities outstanding on February 29, 1924, was $12,521,000,000 (see Appendix C). These securities would be unaffected even by a Constitutional amendment, so that there is no immediate remedy for the situation within the power of Congress except the readjustment of the surtaxes on a basis that will permit capital to seek productive employment and keep it from exhausting itself in tax-exempt securities.

Various measures have been proposed,

both in and out of Congress, for meeting the situation. One proposal was that, instead of passing an amendment to the Constitution permitting taxation by the Federal Government of income from State securities subsequently issued and giving reciprocal rights to the States, a bill should be passed by Congress taxing the income on State and municipal securities now existing and requiring that the statute be not held void without the concurrence of at least all but one of the Supreme Court Justices, and that it shall continue in full force and effect irrespective of the decision of any inferior court.

The general consensus of opinion is that such a bill would be clearly unconstitutional. A digest of the decisions and arguments affecting the question of whether Congress has the power to levy a tax upon the income from securities issued by the States or political subdivisions thereto was made and is set forth in a letter dated January 4, 1924, from Mr. A. W. Gregg, of the Treasury, to the Chairman of the Committee on Ways and

Means of the House of Representatives (see Appendix D).

The measure proposed would apply only to municipal and State securities and would not apply to securities created by Congress. Such discrimination would be indefensible, for it would permit the United States to tax securities issued by a State or its subdivisions but would not allow the State to tax securities issued by the Federal Government.

The proposed Constitutional amendment (H. J. Res. 136), on the other hand, would be reciprocal; that is, both State and United States securities thereafter issued would be taxable. Furthermore, the proposed Constitutional amendment would cover only securities issued subsequently to its adoption and would not affect existing securities in the hands of innocent holders.

Tax exemption was a material factor in fixing the price at which these securities were sold to their present owners. As an example of what this means, the First Liberty 3½'s are fully tax-exempt; the 4¼'s of

ingly urged that action be taken, first, to restrict further issues of tax-exempt securities, in order to block this avenue of escape from the surtaxes, and second, to reduce the surtax rates to a reasonable level, with a maximum of 25%, amounting to 31% when combined with the normal tax. This would provide a workable system and in the long run produce more revenue than the present rates.

The high surtaxes date from the Revenue Act of 1917, and until that time tax-exempt securities presented a problem of but small magnitude since most taxes were levied at level rates and it could generally be said that the loss of taxes was roughly made up by the saving in interest costs. With taxes at flat rates the exemption is worth about as much to one taxpayer as another; and, barring any questions as to conflicting State and Federal jurisdiction, it could be said with some force that, if the State or Federal Governments were to tax the securities which they themselves issued, purchasers of the securities would insist on an interest yield high enough to compensate for the taxes levied. The Federal surtaxes have changed all this and created an entirely different problem. The exemption to which the greatest importance now attaches is the exemption from Federal surtaxes and the value of this exemption depends entirely upon the income of the individual taxpayer. Generally speaking, it will be greatest in the case of the wealthiest taxpayer, while to the person paying only a normal tax or a low surtax the exemption will be relatively of little value. This makes it quite impossible, as a practical matter, for the borrowing State or Federal Government to obtain full value for the exemption carried by the securities, for in the nature of things the securities will be sold in the open market at quoted prices adjusted to market conditions, though to one purchaser the exemption may be worth little or nothing and to another purchaser, who pays the same price, the exemption may be worth the equivalent of 10 or 11% on a taxable security.

Another fundamental difference is that the surtaxes are levied by the Federal Government while the tax-exempt securities are, for the most part, issued by the State and municipal Governments. In other words the Federal Government gets no compensating advantages whatever from any reduction in interest rates that may accrue to the State or municipal Government through the tax-exempt privilege, so that the tax exemption from Federal surtaxes is in fact an involuntary subsidy conferred upon State and municipal Governments by the Federal Government at the expense of its own revenues. It does not meet this objection to say that, whether the State or Federal Governments are involved, it is all one body of taxpayers. While this is undoubtedly a valid argument in support of uniformity of treatment as between the State and Federal Governments, it cannot be advanced in support of a system which permits taxpayers to avoid their taxes to the Federal Government by purchasing securities issued by or under authority of the States.

The facts are that the Federal Government, under the power granted by the 16th amendment to the Constitution of the United States, now levies income taxes on individual incomes, and is imposing graduated additional income taxes, commonly known as surtaxes, on the higher incomes. At the same time the States and municipalities are issuing a growing volume of tax-exempt securities, the income from which is wholly exempt from these very surtaxes, while the Federal Government, though under our present Constitutional system it could itself issue fully tax-exempt securities, has for some years past consistently refrained from issuing such securities in order to protect the public revenues. The Federal Government might change this policy, and by issuing its own securities with full tax exemptions cancel much of the artificial value of State and municipal securities, but this would merely swell the volume of tax-exempt issues and still further endanger the revenues.

It must be clear that graduated additional

income taxes cannot be effective when there
exist side by side with them practically un-
limited quantities of fully tax-exempt securities available to defeat them, and that either
some way must be found to stop the continued issuance of tax-exempt securities or
the Federal Government must find some sub-
stitute for the surtaxes. The issue is immediate and serious, for the yield of the surtaxes
has already been reduced to a relatively small
sum as compared with the early years, and
the persistence of the present system is dis-
torting our whole economic structure and
hampering the development of business and
industry throughout the country. A Constitutional amendment along the lines proposed
in H. J. Res. 136 would correct the situation
and would put State and Federal Governments on an exact equality.

Whatever opposition there is to the proposed amendment to restrict further issues
of tax-exempt securities rests upon a misun-
derstanding of the object and effect of the
amendment, and this, in turn, harks back to

the old controversies about States' rights and
the powers of the Federal Government.
Separated from these old prejudices and
taken from the point of view of the facts as we
have to face them today, the proposed Constitutional amendment involves no question
whatever of States' rights and makes no at-
tack whatever on the credit or borrowing
power of the States or their political subdivisions. The amendment would apply with
absolute equality to the Federal Government,
on the one hand, and the States and their political subdivisions on the other, and the in-
terests of the general welfare would put
exactly the same restrictions upon future
borrowings by the Federal Government as
upon future borrowings by the States and
their political subdivisions. The constantly
growing mass of tax-exempt securities threat-
ens the public revenues, not only of the Federal Government, but of the States as well,
and it is reaching such proportions as to
undermine the development of business and
industry.

The Federal Government, for the most part, has refused to have recourse to tax-exempt issues in financing its own operations, but the volume of tax-exempt securities of the States and their political subdivisions, and of other agencies, already outstanding and currently issued is so large that the value of the exemption to the borrower issuing the securities has become relatively insignificant. Even now the States and their political subdivisions, notwithstanding the full tax exemptions on their securities, are obliged to pay substantially the same rates on their tax-exempt borrowings as the Federal Government pays on securities without exemption from Federal income surtaxes. The facts are that under our system of graduated Federal income surtaxes the issue of tax-exempt securities, while of constantly diminishing advantage to the borrowing State, or city, provides a perfect refuge for wealthy investors, being most valuable to the wealthiest taxpayer. The actuarial figures show that to taxpayers paying surtaxes in the highest brackets securities subject to Federal income surtaxes would have to yield about 12 per cent in order to be as attractive as a 5 per cent tax-exempt security. For this great advantage the State which issues the securities gets but very little compensating return, and certainly no greater return from the wealthiest investor than from the smallest investor (to whom the exemption is relatively worthless), while the United States, which imposes the surtaxes, loses its revenue without any compensating advantage whatever. It is the graduated surtax, of course, that gives the greatest value to the tax exemption; and viewed from this aspect the tax exemption, in substance, constitutes a subsidy from the Federal Government, the cost of which in the long run must fall on those taxpayers who do not or cannot take refuge in tax-exempt securities.

Even from the point of view of the States themselves, it is clear that the continued issuance of tax-exempt securities saves nothing to the taxpayers in the States and that in the long run it brings heavier taxes. The tax-exempt privilege, with the facility that it gives to borrowing, leads in many cases to unnecessary or wasteful public expenditure, and this in turn is bringing about a menacing increase in the debts of States and cities. These debts constitute a constantly growing charge upon the taxpayers in the several States, and will ultimately have to be paid, principal and interest, through tax levies upon these very taxpayers. It is easy to overlook this when the debts are incurred, but it is none the less impossible to escape the facts when the time comes for payment. It is also necessary to bear in mind that in the long run all of these public debts, whether the debts of States and their political subdivisions or of the Federal Government itself, as well as the taxes which must be imposed to meet them, fall upon but one body of taxpayers, and that the apparent advantage of borrowing by States and cities at the expense of the Federal revenues is illusory, since any temporary advantages thus obtained will have to be paid for by the Federal Government at the expense ultimately of the great body of taxpayers. This is particularly true of tax-exempt securities, for their effect is to provide a refuge from taxation for certain classes of taxpayers, with correspondingly higher taxes on all the rest in order to make up the resulting deficiency in the revenues.

Once it is understood no one can raise any valid objection to the proposed Constitutional amendment restricting further issues of tax-exempt securities. As a matter of fact, it is almost grotesque to permit the present anomalous situation to continue, for as things now stand we have on the one hand a system of highly graduated Federal income surtaxes and on the other a constantly growing volume of securities issued by States and cities which are fully exempt from these surtaxes, so that taxpayers have only to buy tax-exempt securities to make the surtaxes ineffective. The only way to correct this condition is by Constitutional amendment, accompanied by a reduction in the rates.

H. J. Res. 136 expressly provides in Section 1 that Federal taxes on income derived from securities, issued after the ratification of the article, by or under the authority of any State, must be without discrimination against income derived from such securities and in favor of income derived from securities issued after the ratification of the article by or under the authority of the United States or any other State. The same protection for the Federal Government is accorded by the second Section, conferring power on the States to lay and collect taxes on income derived from securities issued after the ratification of the article by or under the authority of the United States. Under Section 1 as it stands it would be impossible for the Federal Government to impose an income tax on income from future issues of State or municipal bonds without imposing the same tax on income derived from future issues of its own bonds; and as a practical matter it is almost inconceivable that Congress would be willing to impose such a tax upon the income from both State and Federal securities and at the same time exempt from the tax income derived from securities issued by private corporations. Such a course would be repugnant to every Constitutional principle.

Entirely apart from the practical impossibility of such a situation, however, it is clear that the Constitutional amendment (H. J. Res. 136) would prohibit discrimination against the bonds of a State and in favor of a railroad or industrial corporation. All corporations in this country are organized under either State or Federal law and derive their powers, including the power to borrow money, from charters issued by the State or Federal Governments as the case may be. Securities issued by private corporations, therefore, may be said to be issued "under the authority of" the United States, in the case of a Federal corporation, or the State of incorporation, in the case of a State corporation. Section 1 of the Constitutional amendment expressly prohibits discrimination in favor of securities issued after ratification of the article *under the authority* of the United States or any other State. This in terms would prevent discrimination in favor of any bonds issued by a railroad or industrial corporation incorporated under the laws of the United States or of any other State, and likewise, by a corporation organized under the laws of the State concerned, for it would be Constitutionally impossible for the Federal Government to single out corporations of one State in the granting of tax exemptions. If there were any danger here, however, it could readily be corrected by striking out in the last line of Section 1 the word "other."

Even after the adoption of the proposed Constitutional amendment, neither the United States nor any State would have power to tax securities of the other already issued and outstanding; and under generally accepted Constitutional principles, which have been affirmed by the Supreme Court, the Federal Government cannot levy income taxes upon the salaries of State or municipal officers, nor can the States levy income taxes upon the salaries of Federal officers. To forbid discrimination in favor of these non-taxable sources of income would, in effect, make the Constitutional amendment inoperative. There are also other generally recognized distinctions, as, for example, between earned and unearned income, and miscellaneous special exemptions. These difficulties would embarrass the State Governments, in proceeding under the Constitutional amendment, quite as much as they would the Federal Government, and would make it impossible for the States to levy any income tax upon future issues of Federal securities without at the same time imposing an income tax on all outstanding issues of their own securities, and, in fact, a general income tax upon all sources of income subject to State taxation. Even if it could be Constitutionally done, to levy income taxes upon securities already issued as tax-exempt would constitute a gross breach of faith, while to require a general and uniform income tax, with exactly the same taxation of income from securities as of all other sources of income, would involve almost insuperable practical difficulties and probably prove impossible.

The Constitutional amendment, as drawn in H. J. Res. 136, puts the Federal Government and the States on absolutely the same basis, and the very fact that the Federal Government is ready and willing, for the sake of the general welfare, to place itself under these restrictions as to future issues of tax-exempt securities, notwithstanding its own heavy debt and the practical certainty that it will always have obligations outstanding and to be financed, gives the best possible assurance that the States and their political subdivisions can place themselves under like restrictions without endangering their credit or embarrassing their necessary borrowings.

In proposing a Constitutional amendment, the Federal Government is not asking from the States any more than it is willing to yield for itself. Tax exemption acquires quite a disproportionate value when taxes are not at a level rate but are levied at graduated rates; and the Federal surtaxes are almost wholly responsible for the extraordinary value which tax-exempt securities enjoy today. It is nonsense to refer to this value as something which the States have the right to enjoy in selling their securities, for the value depends in large measure on the relative scarcity of tax-exempt securities and the Federal Government could seriously impair, and nearly destroy, it by issuing all its own securities exempt from surtaxes. Contrariwise, since the value of the exemption turns largely on the existence of graduated surtaxes, the Federal Government could certainly reduce and probably destroy the present premium on tax-exempt securities by changing its own tax system and substituting for the income surtaxes some other form of tax which would not be affected by the presence of tax-exempt securities, as, for example, a tax on sales or expenditures. It may, in fact, be driven to some such change by force of necessity if the present situation continues and enough of the States cling to the privilege of issuing securities that give rich investors the power, at the expense of the rest of the community, to escape from the common burdens of taxation.

The Treasury has strongly recommended that the surtaxes be reduced to a maximum of 25 per cent; that is to say, a maximum combined normal and surtax of 31 per cent. It believes that a revision of the surtaxes on substantially this basis is fundamentally necessary if our present internal revenue system is to be successfully administered. A revision to substantially the basis recommended by the Treasury would correct to some extent the evil of tax-exempt securities, since it would reduce the pressure to escape taxable income, but the evil would none the less remain and would still be serious, at least so long as there were any material graduation of surtax rates. For example, even with a maximum surtax of 25 per cent there would still be a material inducement for large investors to reduce taxable income, and to an investor paying surtaxes at the rate of 25 per cent a fully tax-exempt security would offer substantial advantages as compared with a surtaxable security, while the tax-exempt security would, of course, be far more valuable to such an investor than to a small investor. Lower surtaxes, in other words, would mitigate the evil but would not go to the heart of the situation, for tax exemptions would still persist and tend to defeat any taxes levied at the revised rates.

The Federal Government is issuing each year substantial amounts of new securities and for many years to come will be issuing new securities every year, probably in amounts larger than the aggregate of State and municipal issues during the year, in order to refund its obligations previously issued. Between now and the end of 1928, for example, about $8,000,000,000 of bonds, notes and certificates issued by the Federal

Government will mature and in large measure these maturing obligations will have to be refunded. Any of these refunding obligations issued after the ratification of the Constitutional amendment would be subject to its provisions in the same manner as State or municipal obligations issued after its ratification. The same would be true of other refunding obligations issued by the Federal Government in succeeding years. To show how completely false is the argument referred to above, it is enough to call attention to the fact that the whole war debt of the Federal Government actually matures within the next thirty years, with substantial maturities falling at frequent intervals. These maturing obligations will either be redeemed, in which event the tax exemptions they now carry will cease to be of any importance, or will be refunded into other obligations; and these refunding obligations, if issued after the ratification of the Constitutional amendment, will be subject to its provisions.

Nothing can serve to obscure the main facts in the situation upon which the Treasury relies in urging support for the proposed Constitutional amendment, namely, that the continued issuance of tax-exempt securities is building up a constantly growing mass of privately held property exempt from all taxation; that tax exemption in a democracy such as ours is repugnant to every Constitutional principle, since it tends to create a class in the community which cannot be reached for tax purposes and necessarily increases the burden of taxation on property and incomes that remain taxable; and that it is absolutely inconsistent with any system of graduated income surtaxes to provide at the same time securities which are fully exempt from all taxation, since the exemptions will sooner or later defeat at least all the higher graduations and will always be worth far more to the wealthier taxpayers than to the small ones.

The argument has been advanced that the reduction in the high surtax rate will have no effect upon business, because the most it will mean is simply a shifting of investments, and some one must purchase the tax-exempt securities if they are sold. Before the imposition of the high surtaxes, municipal and State bonds had a wide market. They were well regarded by the investor and found their way into trust funds and into the strong boxes of the conservative investors no longer in active business. Men of initiative and activity did not acquire these securities. Their wealth, therefore, was left free to be devoted to productive business. Under high surtax rates, tax-exempt securities, without risk, afforded a greater net return than productive business with risk could provide, and men with the capacity to produce found it more remunerative to produce nothing. High surtaxes are no more than a bonus at the expense of the Federal Government to the State and municipal borrower, giving a wholly artificial value to tax exemption. This both encourages the municipalities to extravagance and brings into existence in this country a large mass of wealth that cannot be reached for the support of the Government. A removal of the artificial value of tax exemption will restore all securities to natural conditions. True, State and municipal extravagance will be curtailed, but their bonds will sell on their merits to the same class of investors who heretofore favored them. The men capable of business success will get out of their dead investments and put their brains and money to work.

We come back, in the end, to the original argument, that high surtaxes are becoming less and less productive of revenue to the Government and at the same time are injuring business initiative. All business involves risk. If business loses, the Government shares not at all in the loss; if business succeeds, the Government takes more than half the gain. What can long withstand these odds? Capital does not care to take risks on these terms. The spirit of initiative may still be there, but the present high surtaxes are driving it into idleness. America will become a nation of followers, not leaders. There is no escape from the conclusion that a tax system having this inevitable result must be changed.

APPENDIX A

TREASURY DEPARTMENT,
OFFICE OF THE SECRETARY,
Washington, November 10, 1923.

DEAR MR. GREEN:

In accordance with the request which you made shortly after the adjournment of Congress, the Treasury has been engaged for the past few months in considering the possibilities of tax revision and in developing recommendations for the simplification of the law. The situation has developed more favorably than was anticipated, and I am now presenting to you a comprehensive program to which I hope the Committee on Ways and Means will be able to give consideration at the outset of the legislative session.

The fiscal years 1922 and 1923 have each closed with a surplus of about $310,000,000 over and above all expenditures chargeable against ordinary receipts, including the sinking fund and other similar retirements of the debt. This has been possible only through the utmost cooperation between the Executive and Congress, as well as among the executive departments and establishments, all of whom have united in a sincere effort to reduce the expenditures of the Government. At the same time there has been a substantial amount of realization upon securities and other assets remaining over from the war, and the Treasury has succeeded in collecting customs and internal revenue taxes in amounts somewhat exceeding original expectations. The result is that the Government of the United States is firmly established on the basis of having balanced its budget each year since the cessation of hostilities, with a reasonable surplus each year after providing for fixed debt charges like the sinking fund, and stands squarely committed to the policy of including these fixed charges on account of the public debt in its ordinary budget each year, thus assuring an orderly reduction of the war debt out of current revenues.

What has been done during the two years since the establishment of the budget system shows clearly what united effort can accomplish, and gives every reason for hope that the task to which the Administration has set itself for this fiscal year can be successfully performed, namely, the reduction of the ordinary expenditures of the Government to a total of not more than $3,500,000,000, of which about $500,000,000 will be fixed charges on account of the sinking fund and other retirements of the debt. To do this means reductions of about $170,000,000 in the estimates of expenditures submitted by the spending departments and establishments and the exercise of continued pressure all along the line for the utmost economy and efficiency in the operations of the Government.

Having these things in mind, the Treasury has been canvassing the estimates for the present fiscal year and for the succeeding fiscal years with a view to determining on the one hand what further reductions in expenditure it would be safe to count on in developing a tax-revision program, and on the other hand what receipts might reasonably be expected on the basis of existing law, assuming that no changes were to be made in internal taxes. In doing this it has had to keep in mind that under present conditions receipts from customs are abnormally high and that surplus war supplies have now been for the most part liquidated, leaving relatively little to expect on this account in the years to come. It has also had to keep in mind that many of the internal revenue taxes, as, for example, the higher brackets of the surtax, are so rapidly becoming unproductive that it is unsafe to assume that even with no changes in the law the revenues from internal taxes would be maintained. After taking into account all these considerations, and making the most conservative estimates about the yield of existing taxes and the possibilities of further reductions in expenditure, it appears that for this year, and for the next four or five years, there should be a surplus of something over $300,000,000 a year over and above all expenditures chargeable to the ordinary budget, including the fixed debt charges payable out of current revenues. This gives a reasonable margin not merely for tax revision but also for tax reduction.

On this basis the Treasury has the following recommendations to make:

1. *Make a 25 per cent reduction in the tax on earned income.*—The fairness of taxing more lightly income from wages, salaries and

professional services than the income from a business or from investment is beyond question. In the first case, the income is uncertain and limited in duration; sickness or death destroys it and old age diminishes it. In the other, the source of the income continues; it may be disposed of during a man's life and it descends to his heirs. It is estimated that this amendment will mean a loss in revenue of about $97,500,000 a year, the greater part of which falls in the lower income brackets.

2. *Where the present normal tax is 4 per cent reduce it to 3 per cent, and where the present normal tax is 8 per cent reduce it to 6 per cent.*—This affects all personal incomes and the loss of revenue comes largely from the lower brackets. It is estimated that this will mean a loss in revenue of $91,600,000 a year.

3. *Reduce the surtax rates by commencing their application at $10,000 instead of $6,000, and scaling them progressively upwards to 25 per cent at $100,000.*—This will readjust the surtax rates all along the line, and the Treasury recommends the readjustment not in order to reduce the revenues but as a means of saving the productivity of the surtaxes. In the long run it will mean higher

rather than lower revenues from the surtaxes. At the outset it may involve a temporary loss in revenue, but the Government Actuary estimates that even during the first year, if the revision is made early enough, the net loss in revenue from all the changes in the surtaxes would be only about $100,000,000, and that in all probability the revenue from the reduced rates will soon equal or exceed what would accrue at the present rates, because of the encouragement which the changes will give to productive business.

The readjustment of the surtaxes, moreover, is not in any sense a partisan measure. It has been recommended, on substantially this basis, by every Secretary of the Treasury since the end of the war, irrespective of party. The present system is a failure. It was an emergency measure, adopted under the pressure of war necessity and not to be counted upon as a permanent part of our revenue structure. For a short period the surtaxes yielded much revenue, but their productivity has been constantly shrinking and the Treasury's experience shows that the high rates now in effect are progressively becoming less productive of revenue. See Table II, hereto attached. The high rates put pressure on taxpayers to reduce their taxable income, tend to destroy individual initiative and enterprise, and seriously impede the development of productive business. Taxpayers subject to the higher rates can not afford, for example, to invest in American railroads or industries or embark upon new enterprises in the face of taxes that will take 50 per cent or more of any return that may be realized. These taxpayers are withdrawing their capital from productive business and investing it instead in tax-exempt securities and adopting other lawful methods of avoiding the realization of taxable income. The result is to stop business transactions that would normally go through, and to discourage men of wealth from taking the risks which are incidental to the development of new business. Ways will always be found to avoid taxes so destructive in their nature, and the only way to save the situation is to put the taxes on a reasonable basis that will permit business to go on and industry to develop. This, I believe, the readjustment herein recommended will accomplish, and it will not only produce larger revenues but at the same time establish industry and trade on a healthier basis throughout the country. The alternative is a gradual breakdown in the system, and a perversion of industry that stifles our progress as a nation.

The growth of tax-exempt securities, which has resulted directly from the high rates of surtax, is at the same time encouraging extravagance and reckless expenditure on the part of local authorities. These State and local securities will ultimately have to be paid, principal and interest, out of taxes, thus contributing directly to the heavy local taxation which bears so hard on the farmers and small property owners. There is no immediate remedy for this within the power of Congress except the readjustment of the surtaxes on a basis that will permit capital to seek productive employment and keep it from exhausting itself in tax-exempt securities. The productive use of capital in our railroads and industries will also tend to bring lower costs for transportation and manufactured products, thus helping to relieve the farmer from the maladjustment from which he now suffers.

4. *Limit the deduction of capital losses to 12½ per cent of the loss.*—The present revenue law limits the tax on capital gains to 12½ per cent but puts no limit on the capital losses. It is believed it would be sounder

taxation policy generally not to recognize either capital gain or capital loss for purposes of income tax. This is the policy adopted in practically all other countries having income tax laws, but it has not been the policy in the United States. In all probability, more revenue has been lost to the Government by permitting the deduction of capital losses than has been realized by including capital gains as income. So long, however, as our law recognizes capital gains and capital losses for income tax purposes, gain and loss should be placed upon the same basis, and the provision of the 1921 Act taxing capital gains at 12½ per cent should be extended to capital losses, so that the amount by which the tax may be reduced by the capital loss will not exceed 12½ per cent of the loss. It is estimated that this will increase the revenues by about $25,000,000.

5. *Limit the deductions from gross income for interest paid during the year and for losses not of a business character to the amount the sum of these items exceeds tax-exempt income of the taxpayer.*—The 1921 Act provides that interest on indebtedness to acquire or carry tax-exempt securities is not deductible. This provision is ineffective be-

cause a taxpayer may purchase tax-exempt securities for cash and borrow money for other purposes. It is felt also that so long as a taxpayer has income which is not reached for taxation, he should not be permitted to deduct his non-business losses from the income which is taxable, but should be restricted in the first instance to a deduction of these losses from his non-taxable income. The estimated increase of revenue from this source is $35,000,000.

6. *Tax community property income to the spouse having control of the income.*—In some States the income of the husband is a joint income of the husband and wife, and each, therefore, is permitted to file a return for one-half of the income. This gives an unfair advantage to the citizens of those States over the citizens of the other States of this country, and this amendment seeks to restore the equality. It is estimated that it will increase revenues by $8,000,000.

So much for the income tax recommendations, which should become effective January 1, 1924. In order that you may have before you a clear view of the effect of these recommendations as applied to incomes in the various brackets, I am attaching a table, prepared by the Government Actuary, showing the estimated results of the proposed changes in the calendar year 1925, on the basis of the taxable year 1924. The schedule shows a loss of revenue of about $92,000,000 in the brackets under $6,000, and a further loss of revenue of about $52,000,000 in the next bracket of $6,000 to $10,000. In short, about 70 per cent of the reduction would be in the brackets of $10,000 or less, and less than 5 per cent would fall in the brackets over $100,000.

To show the effect of the proposed changes on the income of a typical salaried taxpayer, married and having two children, I call your attention to the following comparative figures:

Income	Present tax	Proposed tax	Saving to taxpayer
$4,000	$28.00	$15.75	$12.25
5,000	68.00	38.25	29.75
6,000	128.00	72.00	56.00
7,000	186.00	99.00	87.00
8,000	276.00	144.00	132.00
9,000	366.00	189.00	177.00
10,000	456.00	234.00	222.00

7. *Repeal the tax on telegrams, telephones and leased wires.*—This is the last of the transportation taxes established during the war, is a source of inconvenience to every person using the telephone or telegraph, and

should now be eliminated from the tax system. This would mean a loss in revenue of about $30,000,000 a year.

8. *Repeal the tax on admissions.*—The greater part of this revenue is derived from the admissions charged by neighborhood moving picture theatres. The tax is, therefore, paid by the great bulk of the people whose main source of recreation is attending the movies in the neighborhood of their homes. This would mean a loss in revenue of about $70,000,000.

9. *Miscellaneous nuisance taxes.*—Your Committee may wish to consider the elimination of various small miscellaneous taxes which have an inconsiderable bearing on the general revenue of the Government, but which are a source of inconvenience to taxpayers and difficult to collect; and possibly there are some articles of jewelry which according to our standard of living cannot properly be denominated luxuries, such as, for instance, ordinary table silver or watches, which you may wish to exempt from the general tax on jewelry. There is not enough margin of revenue available to permit the repeal of the special taxes which are proving productive, but the law could be revised to

good advantage and some of the nuisance taxes repealed without material loss of revenue.

10. In addition to the specific recommendations which directly affect Government revenues, there should be amendments to strengthen the Act and eliminate methods heretofore used by taxpayers to avoid imposition of the tax. The exact amount of additional revenue to the Government which will be brought in by these amendments cannot be estimated, but certainly the amendments will reach much income that heretofore has escaped taxation.

11. *Establish a Board of Tax Appeals in the Treasury but independent of the Bureau of Internal Revenue, to hear and determine cases involving the assessment of internal revenue taxes.*—This will give an independent administrative tribunal equipped to hear both sides of the controversy, which will sit on appeal from the Bureau of Internal Revenue and whose decision will be conclusive on both the Bureau and the taxpayer on the question of assessment. The taxpayer, in the event that decision is against him, will have to pay the tax according to the assessment and have recourse to the courts, while

the Government, in case decision should be against it, will likewise have to have recourse to the courts, in order to enforce collection of the tax.

12. Changes should be made in the present law to simplify administration, make the law more easily understood, and permit a prompt determination of liability in a manner more satisfactory to the taxpayer.

In order that you may see the effect on Government revenues of the above recommendations, I submit the following figures as to the estimated result of these changes:

	Decrease (in millions of dollars)	Increase (in millions of dollars)
Reduction of 25% in tax on earned income	97	..
Reduction in normal tax	92	..
Readjustment of surtax rates	102	..
Capital loss limited to 12½%	..	25
Interest and capital loss deductions limited	..	35
Community property amendment	..	8
Repeal of telegraph and telephone tax	30	..
Repeal of admissions tax	70	..
TOTAL	391	68
	68	
NET LOSS	323	

The benefits of the reduction will be distributed among all classes of taxpayers, and the revision generally will help to free business and industry of vexatious interference and encourage in all lines a more healthy development of productive enterprise.

The present burden of taxation is heavy. The revenues of the Government are sufficient to justify substantial reductions and the people of the country should receive the benefits. No program, however, is feasible if the Government is to be committed to new and extraordinary expenditures. The recommendations for tax reduction set forth in this letter are only possible if the Government keeps within the program of expenditure which the Bureau of the Budget has laid down at the direction of the President. New or enlarged expenditures would quickly eat up the margin of revenue which now appears to be available for reducing the burden of taxation, and to embark on any soldiers' bonus such as was considered in the last Congress or any other program calling for similarly large expenditure would make it necessary to drop all consideration of tax reduction and consider instead ways and means for providing additional revenue. A soldiers' bonus would postpone tax reduction not for one but for many years to come. It would mean an increase rather than a decrease in taxes, for in the long run it could be paid only out of moneys collected by the Government from the people in the form of taxes. Throughout its consideration of the problem the Treasury has proceeded on the theory that the country would prefer a substantial reduction of taxation to the increased taxes that would necessarily follow from a soldiers' bonus, and I have faith to believe that it is justified in that understanding. Certainly there is nothing better calculated to promote the well-being and happiness of the whole country than a measure that will lift, in some degree, the burden of taxation that now weighs so heavily on all.

Very truly yours,

A. W. MELLON,

Secretary of the Treasury.

Hon. WILLIAM R. GREEN,

Acting Chairman, Committee on Ways and Means,

House of Representatives,

Washington, D. C.

TABLE I.—Estimated Effect Upon the Revenue of the Proposed Changes in the Individual Income Tax Law

Income Tax Brackets	Number Paying Tax in Each Bracket	Loss in Tax When All Changes Are in Full Effect. On Income for Calendar Year 1924; Tax Collected 1925						
		Normal tax (Loss)	Surtax (Loss)	Earned income at 75 per cent of rates (Loss)	Capital losses provision (Gain)	Certain deductions limited to nontaxable income (Gain)	Community property provision (Gain)	Net reduction in tax collected
$1,000–$2,000	7,308,200	$64,500,000		$31,250,000	$1,000,000	$2,000,000		$92,750,000
$2,000–$4,000	4,658,200							
$4,000–$6,000	1,158,200							
$6,000–$10,000	558,200	16,100,000	17,500,000	20,000,000	500,000	1,000,000		52,100,000
$10,000–$20,000	228,200	2,000,000	4,400,000	14,000,000	500,000	1,500,000		18,260,000
$20,000–$50,000	80,200	1,300,000	10,100,000	25,000,000	1,000,000	2,500,000	$140,000	30,380,000
$50,000–$100,000	16,500	4,500,000	21,100,000	6,875,000	2,000,000	3,000,000	2,520,000	23,645,000
$100,000–$150,000	3,620	1,300,000	11,100,000	106,000	4,000,000	6,000,000	3,830,000	996,000
$150,000–$200,000	1,430	550,000	6,600,000	69,000	3,000,000	3,500,000	1,510,000	719,000
$200,000–$300,000	840	450,000	7,400,000	56,000	3,000,000	3,500,000		1,406,000
$300,000–$500,000	380	400,000	8,100,000	50,000	3,500,000	3,500,000		1,550,000
$500,000–$1,000,000	150	300,000	7,200,000	44,000	3,000,000	4,000,000		544,000
Over $1,000,000	30	200,000	8,300,000	50,000	3,500,000	4,500,000		550,000
Gain					$25,000,000	$35,000,000	$8,000,000	
Loss		$91,600,000	$101,800,000	$97,500,000				$222,900,000

This table shows the estimated gain or loss in revenue over that estimated under the present law, due to the proposed changes in the Revenue Act of 1921, and allows for the estimated increase in incomes by reason of the readjustment of taxes.

The figures opposite each income tax bracket cover the total estimated receipts within that bracket.

TABLE II. — TABLE SHOWING DECLINE OF TAXABLE INCOMES OVER $300,000.

YEAR	NUMBER OF RETURNS		NET INCOME		DIVIDENDS AND INTEREST ON INVESTMENTS	
	All classes	Incomes over $300,000	All classes	Incomes over $300,000	All classes	Incomes over $300,000
1916	437,036	1,296	$6,298,577,620	$992,972,986	$3,217,348,030	$706,945,738
1917	3,472,890	1,015	13,652,383,207	731,372,153	3,785,557,955	616,119,892
1918	4,425,114	627	15,924,639,355	401,107,868	3,872,234,935	344,111,461
1919	5,332,760	679	19,859,491,448	440,011,589	3,954,553,925	314,984,884
1920	7,259,944	395	23,735,629,183	246,354,585	4,445,145,223	229,052,039
1921	6,662,176	246	19,577,212,528	153,534,305	4,167,291,294	165,370,228

APPENDIX B

NET INCOME	SINGLE PERSON		MARRIED PERSON WITH TWO DEPENDENT CHILDREN	
	Present law	Proposed	Present law	Proposed
$1,200	$8	$4.50	..	..
1,400	16	9.00	..	..
1,600	24	13.50	..	..
1,800	32	18.00	..	..
2,000	40	22.50	..	..
2,200	48	27.00	..	..
2,400	56	31.50	..	..
2,600	64	36.00	..	..
2,800	72	40.50	..	..
3,000	80	45.00	..	..
3,200	88	49.50	..	..
3,400	96	54.00	$4	$2.25
3,600	104	58.50	12	6.75
3,800	112	63.00	20	11.25
4,000	120	67.50	28	15.75
4,200	128	72.00	36	20.25
4,400	136	76.50	44	24.75
4,600	144	81.00	52	29.25
4,800	152	85.50	60	33.75
5,000	160	90.00	68	38.25
5,200	176	99.00	96	54.00
5,400	192	108.00	104	58.50
5,600	208	117.00	112	63.00
5,800	224	126.00	120	67.50
6,000	240	135.00	128	72.00

INCOME TAX ON EARNED INCOMES FROM $1,200 TO $6,000

NET INCOME	SINGLE PERSON		MARRIED PERSON WITHOUT DEPENDENT CHILDREN	
	Present law	Proposed	Present law	Proposed
$1,200	$8	$4.50	..	..
1,400	16	9.00	..	..
1,600	24	13.50	..	..
1,800	32	18.00	..	..
2,000	40	22.50	..	..
2,200	48	27.00	..	..
2,400	56	31.50	..	..
2,600	64	36.00	$4	$2.25
2,800	72	40.50	12	6.75
3,000	80	45.00	20	11.25
3,200	88	49.50	28	15.75
3,400	96	54.00	36	20.25
3,600	104	58.50	44	24.75
3,800	112	63.00	52	29.25
4,000	120	67.50	60	33.75
4,200	128	72.00	68	38.25
4,400	136	76.50	76	42.75
4,600	144	81.00	84	47.25
4,800	152	85.50	92	51.75
5,000	160	90.00	100	56.25
5,200	176	99.00	128	72.00
5,400	192	108.00	136	76.50
5,600	208	117.00	144	81.00
5,800	224	126.00	152	85.50
6,000	240	135.00	160	90.00

INCOME TAX PAYABLE UPON CERTAIN EARNED NET INCOMES

NET INCOME	SINGLE PERSON		HEAD OF FAMILY WITH TWO DEPENDENT CHILDREN	
	Present law	Proposed	Present law	Proposed
$1,000	$0.00	$0.00	$0.00	$0.00
2,000	40.00	22.50	0.00	0.00
3,000	80.00	45.00	0.00	0.00
4,000	120.00	67.50	28.00	15.75
5,000	160.00	90.00	68.00	38.25
6,000	240.00	135.00	128.00	72.00
7,000	330.00	180.00	186.00	99.00
8,000	420.00	225.00	276.00	144.00
9,000	510.00	270.00	366.00	189.00
10,000	600.00	315.00	456.00	234.00
11,000	700.00	367.50	556.00	286.50
12,000	800.00	420.00	656.00	339.00
13,000	910.00	480.00	766.00	399.00
14,000	1,020.00	540.00	876.00	459.00
15,000	1,140.00	607.50	996.00	526.50
16,000	1,260.00	675.00	1,116.00	594.00
17,000	1,390.00	750.00	1,246.00	669.00
18,000	1,520.00	825.00	1,376.00	744.00
19,000	1,660.00	907.50	1,516.00	826.50
20,000	1,800.00	990.00	1,656.00	909.00
21,000	1,960.00	1,080.00	1,816.00	999.00
22,000	2,120.00	1,170.00	1,976.00	1,089.00
23,000	2,290.00	1,267.50	2,146.00	1,186.50
24,000	2,460.00	1,365.00	2,316.00	1,284.00
25,000	2,640.00	1,470.00	2,496.00	1,389.00

TABLE SHOWING THE TOTAL TAX PAYABLE UPON CERTAIN INCOMES UNDER THE RATES OF THE PRESENT LAW AND UNDER THE SUGGESTED RATES

NET INCOME	SINGLE PERSON UNEARNED INCOME		MARRIED MAN WITH TWO DEPENDENTS UNEARNED INCOME	
	Present law	Proposed law	Present law	Proposed law
$30,000	$3,600	$2,720	$3,456	$2,612
40,000	5,920	4,600	5,776	4,492
50,000	8,720	6,740	8,576	6,632
100,000	30,220	19,900	30,076	19,792
150,000	58,220	35,400	58,076	35,292
200,000	86,720	50,900	86,576	50,792
250,000	115,720	66,400	115,576	66,292
300,000	144,720	81,900	144,576	81,792
400,000	202,720	112,900	202,576	112,792
500,000	260,720	143,900	260,576	143,792
1,000,000	550,720	298,900	550,576	298,792

APPENDIX C

Treasury Department
April 5, 1924.

ESTIMATED AMOUNT OF WHOLLY TAX-EXEMPT SECURITIES OUTSTANDING FEBRUARY 29, 1924
(*Revised basis*) [1]

ISSUED BY	GROSS AMOUNT	AMOUNT HELD IN TREASURY OR IN SINKING FUNDS	AMOUNT HELD OUTSIDE OF TREASURY AND SINKING FUNDS
States, counties, cities, etc. . . .	$11,378,000,000	$1,707,000,000 [2]	$9,671,000,000
Territories, insular possessions, and District of Columbia	125,000,000	20,000,000 [3]	105,000,000
United States Government . . .	2,294,000,000	755,000,000 [4]	1,539,000,000
Federal land banks, intermediate credit banks, and joint stock land banks	1,310,000,000	104,000,000 [5]	1,206,000,000
Total Feb. 29, 1924	$15,107,000,000	$2,586,000,000	$12,521,000,000
Comparative totals:			
December 31, 1923	$14,885,000,000	$2,564,000,000	$12,321,000,000
December 31, 1922	13,652,000,000	2,331,000,000	11,321,000,000
December 31, 1918	9,506,000,000	1,799,000,000	7,707,000,000
December 31, 1912	5,554,000,000	1,468,000,000	4,086,000,000

[1] Since issuing the estimate of January 1, 1924, the method of estimating has been revised and as a result both the gross amount of securities outstanding and the amount held in sinking funds have been substantially increased but the net amount outstanding except for the normal growth has been changed but slightly.

[2] Total amount of State and local sinking funds.

[3] Total amount of sinking funds and amount held in trust by the Treasurer of the United States.

[4] Amount held in trust by the Treasurer of the United States.

[5] See Note (4), also partly owned by the United States Government.

The Growth of Tax-Exempt Securities in the United States

The amount of State and local securities outstanding in the United States has increased with greater rapidity than the amount of corporate and other securities (exclusive of United States Government securities) during the past few years, as shown in the following tables:

TABLE I. — TOTAL SECURITIES FLOATED IN THE UNITED STATES, TOTAL STATE AND LOCAL SECURITIES, AND PER CENT OF STATE AND LOCAL TO TOTAL 1912–1923

(000,000 *omitted*)

YEAR	TOTAL SECURITIES FLOATED IN THE UNITED STATES (EXCLUSIVE OF U.S. GOV'T OBLIGATIONS)	TOTAL STATE AND LOCAL SECURITIES FLOATED IN THE UNITED STATES	PER CENT OF STATE AND LOCAL TO TOTAL
1912 . . .	$3,952 [1]	$387	9.79
1913 . . .	2,952 [1]	403	13.65
1914 . . .	2,998 [1]	474	15.81
1915 . . .	3,998 [1]	499	12.48
1916 . . .	5,438 [1]	457	8.40
1917 . . .	3,641 [1]	451	12.39
1918 . . .	2,877 [1]	297	10.32
1919 . . .	4,286	692	16.15
1920 . . .	4,010	683	17.03
1921 . . .	4,204	1,209	28.76
1922 . . .	5,245	1,102	21.01
1923 . . .	4,986	1,032	20.70

[1] The figures of total securities floated in the United States 1912–1918 are estimates made by the Harvard University Committee on Economic Research based upon data from various sources. They are supposed to include both foreign and domestic securities, new and refunding, floated in the United States during the period in question. All other figures are taken from the *Commercial and Financial Chronicle*.

TABLE II. — New Capital Issues of Corporations and States and Municipalities in the United States 1913–1923

YEAR	AMOUNTS		INDEX NUMBERS (1919 BASIS)	
	Corporate Securities	State and Local Securities	Corporate Securities	State and Local Securities
1913	$1,646,000,000	$376,234,691	71	55
1914	1,437,000,000	464,727,871	62	69
1915	1,435,000,000	466,433,730	62	69
1916	2,187,000,000	433,735,031	95	64
1917	1,530,000,000	435,873,593	66	64
1918	1,345,000,000	286,831,077	58	42
1919	2,303,328,636	678,187,262	100	100
1920	2,710,011,386	671,765,574	118	99
1921	1,823,004,851	1,199,396,561	79	177
1922	2,335,734,207	1,070,901,057	101	158
1923	2,730,796,155	1,013,786,164	119	149

Corporate issues 1913–1918 from *Review of Economic Statistics* (Harvard University Press), May 25, 1921, p. 98. Includes both new and refunding issues; these figures include only those which have been reported and not additional estimates. All other figures from the *Commercial and Financial Chronicle*.

Table I shows that State and local securities have constituted a much larger proportion of the securities floated in the United States since 1919 than they did in earlier years. Table II differs from Table I in that only corporate securities have been used in the first column and that refunding issues have been omitted wherever possible. In the eleven years shown the amount of State and local securities issued annually has increased with greater rapidity than the amount of corporate securities. The index numbers show that the great increase in the State and local securities issued in the last three years has not been paralleled by issues of corporate securities.

TABLE III. — ESTIMATED AMOUNT OF WHOLLY TAX-EXEMPT SECURITIES IN THE UNITED STATES, EXCLUSIVE OF THOSE HELD IN TREASURY, SINKING AND TRUST FUNDS. 1912–1923 [1]

DECEMBER 31	TAX EXEMPT-SECURITIES
1912	$4,086,000,000
1913	4,338,000,000
1914	4,789,000,000
1915	5,188,000,000
1916	5,623,000,000
1917	7,994,000,000
1918	7,707,000,000 [2]
1919	8,506,000,000 [3]
1920	9,804,000,000
1921	10,586,000,000
1922	11,321,000,000
1923	12,309,000,000

[1] The figures for State and local debt for 1912 and 1922 are based on the Census compilations. For the intermediate year interpolations have been made on the basis of annual issues. The actual amounts of Federal Government and Farm loan tax-exempt issues have been added to the estimates for each year.

[2] The decline in 1918 was due to the fact that very few State and local bonds were issued, and over half a billion of wholly tax-exempt First Liberty 3½ per cent bonds were converted during the year to 4's or 4¼'s which are not wholly tax exempt.

[3] This does not include the Victory 3¾ per cent notes outstanding, as separate figures for the Victory 3¾'s and 4¾'s were not available for 1919. The Victory 3¾'s are included in 1920 and 1921, but not in 1922, as they matured before the end of the year.

Table III includes all wholly tax-exempt securities outstanding except those in the

United States Treasury, sinking funds and trust funds. Both in 1912 and in 1922 the State and local securities composed about three-fourths of the total tax-exempt securities outstanding. Reliable figures as to the amounts of all other securities outstanding are not available.

APPENDIX D

The letter from Mr. A. W. Gregg, Assistant
to the Secretary of the Treasury, is, in part,
as follows:

January 4, 1924.

Hon. W. R. GREEN,
Chairman Ways and Means Committee,
House of Representatives.

MY DEAR MR. CHAIRMAN: Prior to its adjournment before the holidays the committee
requested that I prepare for the assistance
of the committee a digest of the decisions
and arguments affecting the question of
whether Congress has the power to levy a tax
upon the income from securities issued by
States or political subdivisions thereof. In
accordance with that request the following is
submitted.

Two questions will be considered, (1)
whether the Federal Government has the gen-

eral power to lay a tax upon income derived from securities issued by States or political subdivisions thereof; (2) in the event that Congress may not lay a tax upon income from all such securities, whether the income from any obligation issued by States or political subdivisions thereof may be taxed by the Federal Government.

The earliest decision of the Supreme Court upon the question of the power of the United States to tax State instrumentalities is The Collector *v*. Day (1870), 11 Wall. 113. Under the Civil War income tax acts a tax was assessed on the salary of Hay, a probate judge in Massachusetts. He paid the tax under protest and brought action to recover it. It was held by the Supreme Court that Congress had no power to impose a tax upon the salary of a State judicial officer. The court cited Dobbins *v*. Commissioners (1842), 16 Pet. 435; McCulloch *v*. Maryland (1819), 4 Wheat. 316; and Weston *v*. Charleston (1829), 2 Pet. 449, as establishing the proposition "that the State governments can not lay a tax upon the constitutional means employed by the Government of the Union to execute its constitutional powers," and concluded that, on the same principle, the United

All of this has laid the foundation for national tax reduction and reform. In time of war finances, like all else, must yield to national defense and preservation. In time of peace finances, like all else, should minister to the general welfare. Immediately upon my taking office it was determined after conference with Secretary Mellon that the Treasury Department should study the possibility of tax reduction for the purpose of securing relief to all taxpayers of the country and emancipating business from unreasonable and hampering exactions. The result was the proposed bill, which is now pending before the Congress. It is doubtful if any measure ever received more generous testimony of approval. Opposition has appeared to some of its details, but to the policy of immediate and drastic reduction of taxes, so arranged as to benefit all classes and all kinds of business, there has been the most general approbation. These recommendations have been made by the Treasury as the expert financial adviser of the Government. They follow, in their main principle of a decrease in high surtaxes, which is only another name for war taxes, the views of the two preceding Secretaries of the Treasury, both of them Democrats of pronounced ability. They are non-partisan, well thought out, and sound. They carry out the policy of reducing the taxes of everybody, especially people of moderate income. They give to the country almost a million dollars every working day.

The proposed bill maintains the fixed policy of rates graduated in proportion to ability to pay. That policy has received almost universal sanction. It is sustained by sound arguments based on economic, social, and moral grounds. But in taxation, like everything else, it is necessary to test a theory by practical results. The first object of taxation is to secure revenue. When the taxation of large incomes is approached with that in view, the problem is to find a rate which will produce the largest returns. Experience does not show that the higher rate produces the larger revenue. Experience is all in the other way. When the surtax rate on incomes of $300,000 and over was but 10 per cent, the revenue was about the same as when it was at 65 per cent. There is no escaping the fact that when the taxation of large incomes is excessive, they tend to disappear. In 1916 there were 206 incomes of $1,000,000 or more. Then the high tax rate went into effect.

The next year there were only 141, and in 1918 but 67. In 1919 the number declined to 65. In 1920 it fell to 33, and in 1921 it was further reduced to 21. I am not making any argument with the man who believes that 55 per cent ought to be taken away from the man with $1,000,000 income, or 68 per cent from a $5,000,000 income; but when it is considered that in the effort to get these amounts we are rapidly approaching the point of getting nothing at all, it is necessary to look for a more practical method. That can be done only by a reduction of the high surtaxes when viewed solely as a revenue proposition, to about 25 per cent.

I agree perfectly with those who wish to relieve the small taxpayer by getting the largest possible contribution from the people with large incomes. But if the rates on large incomes are so high that they disappear, the small taxpayer will be left to bear the entire burden. If, on the other hand, the rates are placed where they will produce the most revenue from large incomes, then the small taxpayer will be relieved. The experience of the Treasury Department and the opinion of the best experts place the rate which will collect most from the people of great wealth, thus giving the largest relief to people of moderate wealth, at not over 25 per cent.

A very important social and economic question is also involved in high rates. That is the result taxation has upon national development. Our progress in that direction depends upon two factors—personal ability and surplus income. An expanding prosperity requires that the largest possible amount of surplus income should be invested in productive enterprise under the direction of the best personal ability. This will not be done if the rewards of such action are very largely taken away by taxation. If we had a tax whereby on the first working day the Government took 5 per cent of your wages, on the second day 10 per cent, on the third day 20 per cent, on the fourth day 30 per cent, on the fifth day 50 per cent, and on the sixth day 60 per cent, how many of you would continue to work on the last two days of the week? It is the same with capital. Surplus income will go into tax-exempt securities. It will refuse to take the risk incidental to embarking in business. This will raise the rate which established business will have to pay for new capital, and result in a marked